JUST
POCKETS

JUST POCKETS

Sewing Techniques and Design Ideas

PATRICIA MOYES

The Taunton Press

Cover photos: Jack Deutsch

Taunton
BOOKS & VIDEOS
for fellow enthusiasts

Text © 1997 by Patricia Moyes
Photos © 1997 by The Taunton Press
Illustrations © 1997 by The Taunton Press

Printed in the United States of America
10 9 8 7 6 5 4 3 2 1

A THREADS Book
THREADS® is a trademark of The Taunton Press, Inc.,
registered in the U.S. Patent and Trademark Office.

The Taunton Press, Inc., 63 South Main Street, P.O. Box 5506,
Newtown, CT 06470-5506
e-mail: tp@taunton.com

Library of Congress Cataloging-in-Publication Data

Moyes, Patricia.
    Just pockets : sewing techniques and design ideas / Patricia Moyes.
        p.   cm.
    Includes index.
    ISBN 1-56158-170-4
    1. Pockets 2. Dressmaking. 3. Sewing. I. Title.
    TT552.M63   1997   97-13757
646.4—dc21   CIP

Sandra, Marcy, Shermane. Septina, Miren, Lynn. Teachers and friends, these women helped me realize this project. I dedicate this book to them, with affection.

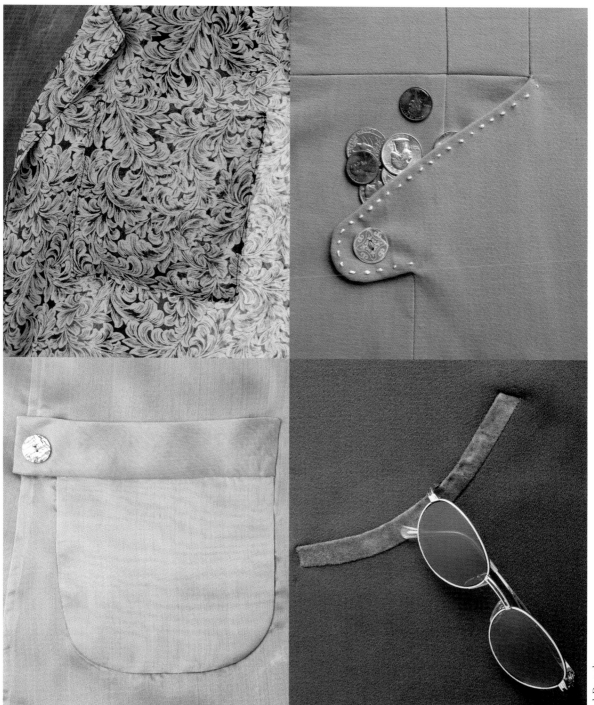

CONTENTS

INTRODUCTION

Hands stuffed down into deep welt pockets of a trench coat, collar turned up, hat pulled low—images of Humphrey Bogart in *Casablanca*. Granddad pulling his gold watch from a small vest pocket as his excited grand-children look on. A three-year-old playing in her favorite skirt—a blue chambray circle skirt with two patch pockets trimmed with eyelet and pink ribbon roses. Wrapping a coin in a tissue and tucking it into your pants pocket before going to the movies. Aunt Julie's lace-edged hanky draping from the breast pocket of her navy linen suit.

Pockets—places to put your hands and your things, details that enhance design. I think pockets are wonderful. Start noticing pocket details and con-struction, and you'll think so too.

Pockets can be simple additions to easy-to-make garments, adding just the right touch of style. Pockets can enhance great garments—where would haute couture be without its remarkable seaming that wondrously ends at a great pocket, its oversize, oddly sized, or unbe-lievably placed pockets? Couture's super tailors manage to coax pockets into the most sensuous fabrics. And we, the home sewers and the clothes lovers, want the very same pockets in the very same fabrics in our closets. If we can't shop for the clothes, we shop for the details, usually from top-of-the-line ready-to-wear (why waste time copying what's already been copied?), then apply those same details to our own creations. Of course we want our pockets con-structed as expertly as ready-to-wear (or maybe better), so creating those great pocket details at home becomes the challenge.

I believe a poorly sewn pocket is the mark of a home-sewn garment—the kind of garment that screams HOME-MADE! I don't want any of those in my closet—and you shouldn't either!

So this book is about great pockets and about making great pockets. Pocket construction in general requires a range of skills and attention to detail, and my goal was to combine the best how-to information with the best pocket styles—giving you a single sourcebook for all the great pockets.

Whether you are relatively new to sewing or an advanced sewer, *Just Pockets* has something for you. If you only open a book for a cursory check of the step-by-step instructions, the clearly detailed drawings will provide you with a handy outline. The fun and fabulous pocket styles included are to inspire you to try something different. For the beginner and intermediate sewer, *Just Pockets* will be your guide—clear instructions for lots of pockets are here for you to follow, to build your skills for successful pocket constructions.

As the world of pockets unfolds in the following pages, I encourage you to try something new, try something harder, don't make what the pattern dictates—explore the possibilities of a new pocket style. You'll find that you'll be as fascinated about pockets as I am.

Jack Deutsch

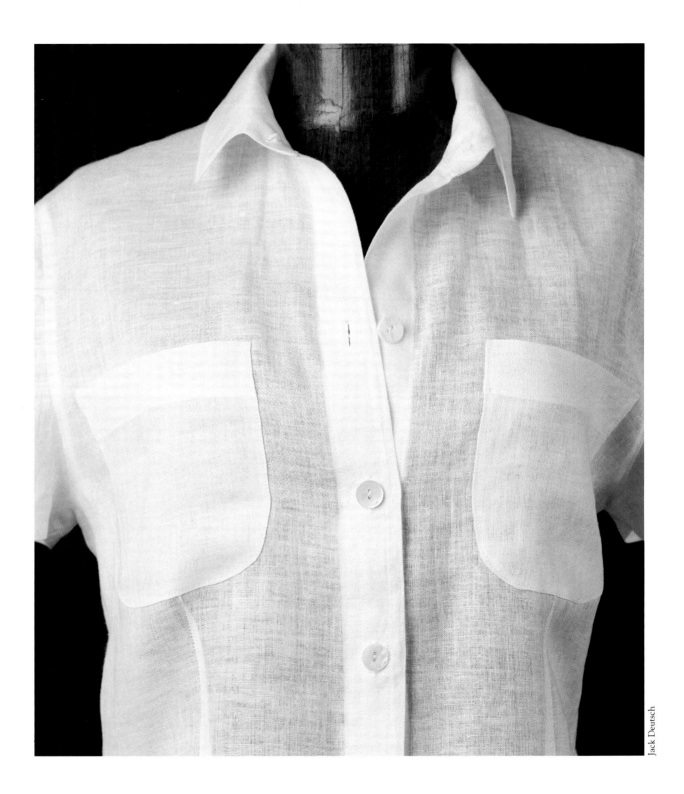

2

PATCH POCKETS

Patch pockets grace every style and type of garment—shirts, jackets, skirts, and pants. They appear on garment tops, bottoms, fronts, backs, and sides. They can hang free, or they can be topstitched or decoratively stitched down. Patch pockets can be unlined, lined, piped, buttoned down, fringed, shaped, or banded.

Although patch pockets appear simple, it takes practice to make them so they don't look homemade. A couple of basics apply to every type. First, because a patch pocket is stitched to the garment from the right side, pocket placement should be marked on the garment with tailor tacks at the top corners, instead of with chalk or marking pens, which may leave visible traces (see the photo below left). And second, if your garment requires two patch pockets—one on each side of a shirt or jacket, for instance—both pockets should be worked at the same time and compared *before* they're placed on the garment. If they don't match, it's easiest to make changes before they're stitched in place.

In this chapter, you'll learn to make a wide range of patch pockets. Let's start with the most basic, and progress through variations that require increasing levels of skill.

UNLINED PATCH POCKETS

The unlined patch pocket with a foldback facing is the simplest. A typical commercial garment pattern will provide a single pocket piece, which you attach to the garment by topstitching along three sides of the pocket. You must mark the pocket placement on the garment, finish the top edge of the pocket, then sew the pocket to the garment.

1. Mark the foldback line at the top of the pocket piece. I usually make a small snip at each end of the line, but you can use chalk or a marking pen at the edges because they will be turned under with the seam allowances.

2. Finish the top edge of the pocket piece. Use an overlock stitch or turn the edge under ¼ in. and stitch it down.

3. With the pocket piece right side up, fold the top of the pocket toward the right side along the foldline and press. Measure the foldback to be sure it's even all the way across (see the photo below right). If you're making two pockets, compare them. Pin or baste the foldback.

4. Stitch around the edges of the pocket piece, anchoring the foldback in place on each side. Because I use the standard American seam allowance of ⅝ in., I sew ⅝ in. from the edges with a normal stitch length and shorten my stitches in the foldback areas. The stitching line becomes the guideline for making neat, matching pockets.

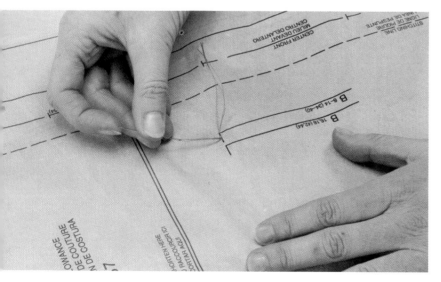

Use tailor tacks to mark pocket placement.

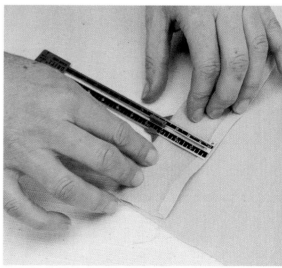

Measure the foldback carefully.

If your pocket has straight edges, you can either machine-stitch neat, square corners or sew straight to each edge of the pocket piece and begin again along the adjoining edge. If the pocket is curved, use the stay-stitch-plus technique for easy, even curves: Place your finger firmly behind the presser foot so the fabric crimps up against it and gathers somewhat (see the photo at right).

5. Trim the seam allowances in the foldback to eliminate bulk. Turn the foldback right side out, and use a point turner to push out the corners (see the drawing below). Press all edges to the wrong side, using your stitching lines as guides.

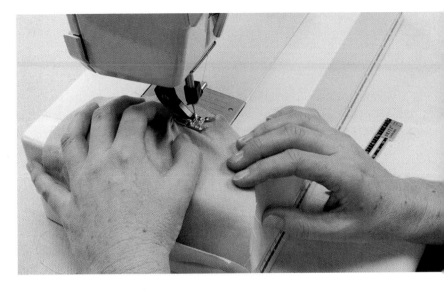

Use stay-stitch-plus to help ease curves.

FINISHING THE PATCH POCKET

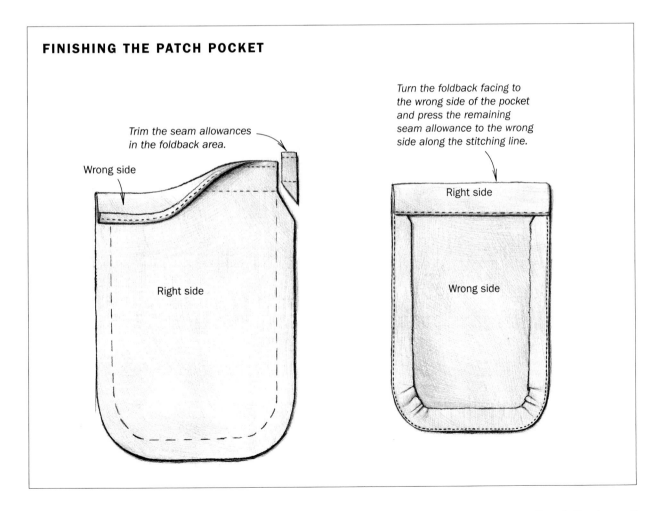

Trim the seam allowances in the foldback area.

Wrong side

Right side

Turn the foldback facing to the wrong side of the pocket and press the remaining seam allowance to the wrong side along the stitching line.

Right side

Wrong side

Using a Template

Teacher/designer Shermane Fouché taught me how to use a template to make a curved patch pocket. Since it's otherwise difficult to match the edges of a curved patch pocket, this is my favorite technique. It works equally well on square and rectangular pockets.

Use a tracing wheel and tracing paper to trace the finished pocket from the pattern piece onto a manila file folder or paper of the same weight (see the top photo below). Carefully cut out the template and fold it in half to make sure the edges and corners are even (see the bottom photo below). The object is to do your fussing before pressing.

Finish the top edge of the pocket piece.

Place a large piece of tissue paper on the ironing board, then place the fabric pocket piece right

Use tracing paper and a tracing wheel to transfer the pattern onto stiff paper or a file folder.

Check to be sure the template edges are even.

side down on top of it. Place the template on top of the pocket. Align the top of the template with the top of the pocket, and center it so the seam allowances are evenly visible around the remaining sides (see the top photo below).

Carefully pull all of the edges of the tissue paper toward the center of the template. You are actually using the tissue paper to gather the seam allowances over the edges of the template. I am not neat when I do this—I have a fistful of tissue—although I am careful to pull the seam allowances tightly into posi-tion. Use a hot steam iron to give the edges of the package a good shot of steam (see the bottom photo below).

Remove the tissue and template, and *voilà*—you have a perfectly shaped pocket. Sew it to the gar-ment as usual.

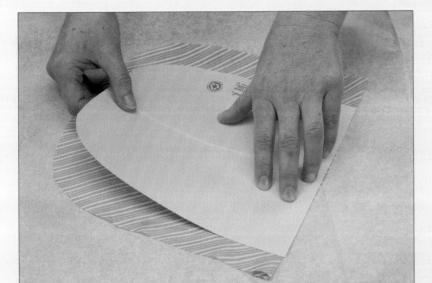

Align the top edge of the template with the finished edge of the pocket.

Set the edges with plenty of steam.

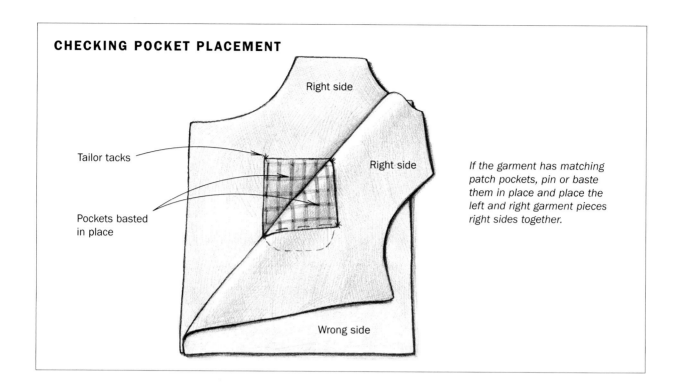

CHECKING POCKET PLACEMENT

Right side

Tailor tacks

Right side

Pockets basted
in place

If the garment has matching patch pockets, pin or baste them in place and place the left and right garment pieces right sides together.

Wrong side

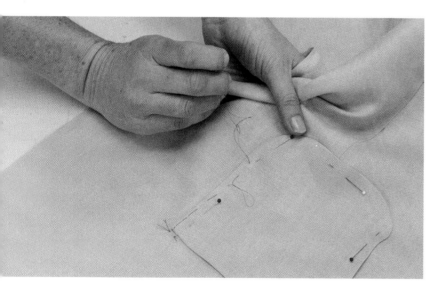

Hand-baste the pocket to the garment before topstitching.

6. Pin the completed pocket on the right side of the garment, aligning the upper corners with your tailor tacks. If the garment has matching patch pockets, check their placement by placing the right garment piece against the left garment piece, matching all edges (see the drawing above). Use pins and your fingers to be sure the pockets are symmetrical—not just along the top, but all the way around. Reposition the pockets if necessary. Baste in place (see the photo at left).

You can skip the basting step if you have sewn enough patch pockets to accurately attach a pocket without it. Certain fabrics, such as silks, other slippery fabrics, and bulky jacket weights, warrant basting regardless of your skill. If you're a fussy sewer, as I am, hand-

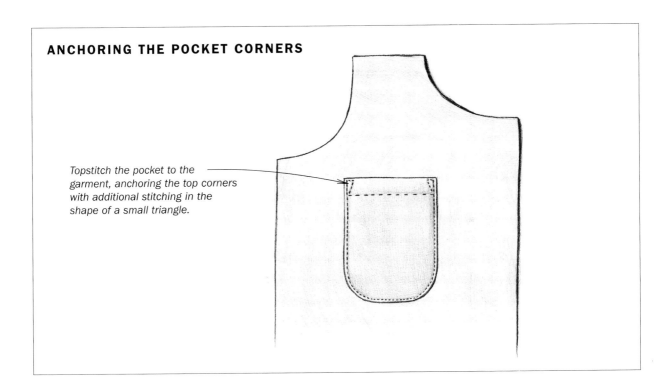

ANCHORING THE POCKET CORNERS

Topstitch the pocket to the garment, anchoring the top corners with additional stitching in the shape of a small triangle.

baste your pockets in place regardless of the fabric, making ½-in. running stitches ¼ in. from the pocket edges. I find that basting allows me to concentrate on close, neat edgestitching without worrying about whether the pocket will move as I sew it down.

7. Machine-stitch the pocket in place from the right side, close to the pocket edge. Anchor the foldback area on each edge with additional stitching in the shape of a small triangle (see the drawing above). This is the area that gets the most stress, and your pocket is less likely to pull away from the garment if you reinforce it this way.

8. Trimming, though not always necessary with a rectangular patch, is especially important on a curved pocket. Turn the pocket inside out. *Carefully*

trim away ⅜ in. of the seam allowance, remembering that if you slip you will cut the pocket or the garment. Turn the pocket right side out again and press.

LINED PATCH POCKETS

One rung up the ladder of difficulty from the basic patch is the lined patch pocket. Lining a patch pocket is easy and preferred for all but the quickest jackets. For a fully lined pocket, you need a lining piece that's the same size as the pocket piece; for a lined pocket with a foldback facing, you need a lining piece that's the size of the pocket piece *minus* the size of the foldback facing plus seam allowance (see the drawing on p. 10).

FULLY LINED PATCH POCKET

1. Trim 1/16 in. from the sides and bottom of the lining piece. Don't trim the top. Making the lining piece a bit smaller than the pocket piece prevents the lining from showing from the right side.

2. With right sides together, stitch the lining piece to the pocket piece across the top. Open the pieces out and press the seam allowance toward the pocket piece.

3. With right sides together, fold the lining piece back down against the pocket piece, matching and pinning the remaining edges. Stitch around the three sides, leaving an opening of 1½ in. at the bottom (see the drawing on the facing page). Remember, because you have trimmed the lining piece, it is slightly smaller than the pocket piece, but you must still match the edges as you sew. Work with the pocket side down—the feed dogs will help ease the pieces together.

CUTTING THE PIECES FOR A LINED POCKET

FULLY LINED PATCH POCKET

Pocket piece

Lining piece

Pocket and lining pieces are the same size.

LINED PATCH POCKET WITH FOLDBACK FACING

Pocket piece

Lining piece

Lining piece is smaller than the pocket piece by the amount of the foldback plus seam allowance.

4. Trim the seam allowances close to the stitching. Turn the pocket right side out through the hole in the bottom, using a point turner to push the corners out. Press.

5. Following steps 6 and 7 for the unlined patch pocket (see pp. 8-9), position and stitch your perfectly lined patch pocket in place. You can sew close to the edge of the pocket, anchoring the corners with triangular or double stitching, or you can topstitch the pocket away from the edge. The latter is a nice alternative to edgestitching.

LINED PATCH POCKET WITH FOLDBACK FACING

1. Mark the foldback line at the top of the pocket piece by making a small snip at each end.

2. Trim $\frac{1}{16}$ in. from the sides and bottom of the lining piece. Don't trim the top. Making the lining piece a bit smaller than the pocket piece prevents the lining from showing when the pocket is assembled.

3. With right sides together, stitch the lining piece to the pocket piece across the top, leaving an opening of $1\frac{1}{2}$ in. in the center of the seam (see the drawing on p. 12). Press the seam allowance open.

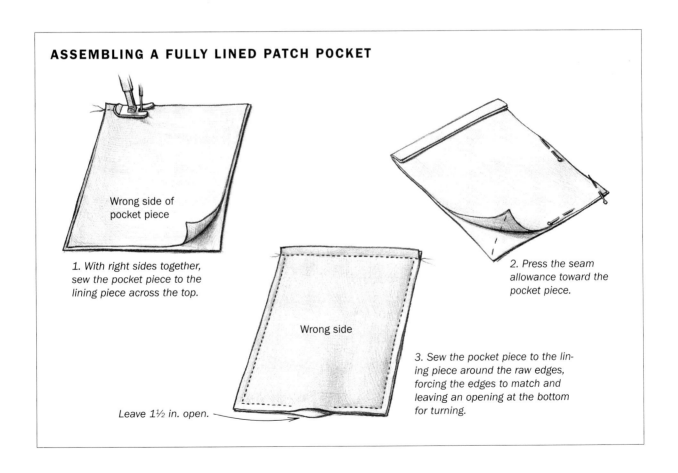

ASSEMBLING A FULLY LINED PATCH POCKET

Wrong side of pocket piece

1. With right sides together, sew the pocket piece to the lining piece across the top.

2. Press the seam allowance toward the pocket piece.

Wrong side

Leave 1½ in. open.

3. Sew the pocket piece to the lining piece around the raw edges, forcing the edges to match and leaving an opening at the bottom for turning.

ASSEMBLING A LINED PATCH POCKET WITH FOLDBACK FACING

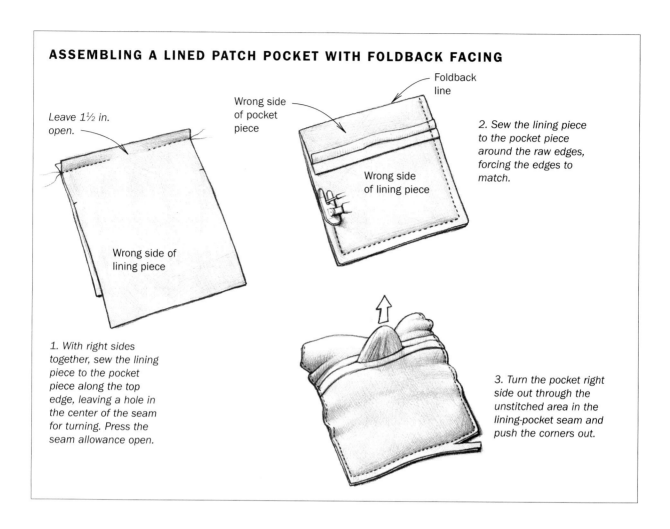

Leave 1½ in. open.

Wrong side of pocket piece

Foldback line

Wrong side of lining piece

2. Sew the lining piece to the pocket piece around the raw edges, forcing the edges to match.

Wrong side of lining piece

1. With right sides together, sew the lining piece to the pocket piece along the top edge, leaving a hole in the center of the seam for turning. Press the seam allowance open.

3. Turn the pocket right side out through the unstitched area in the lining-pocket seam and push the corners out.

4. With right sides together, fold the pocket-and-lining piece in half along the foldback line, using the snips as a guide. Match and pin the side and bottom edges. Stitch around the three edges. Remember, because you have trimmed the lining piece, it is slightly smaller than the pocket piece, but you must still match the edges as you sew. Work with the pocket side down—the feed dogs will help ease the pieces together.

5. Trim the seam allowances close to the stitching. Turn the pocket right side out through the hole in the seam allowance, using a point turner to push the corners out (see the drawing above). Press.
6. Following steps 6 and 7 for the unlined patch pocket (see pp. 8-9), position and edgestitch or topstitch the pocket to your garment, reinforcing the top corners.

Using Plaids and Bias

Plaid patch pockets cut on the bias look great. Use bias when you want your pockets to have a different look or when it may be difficult to match the plaid, check, or stripe. The secret to working successfully with bias is to cut each piece to accommodate the stretching that will inevitably occur.

Cut a piece of fabric larger than you need for the pocket. Take it to the ironing board and start pressing (see the photo below). Press a lot. Press the bias in all directions, using the iron to stretch the fabric as much as you can. Let the piece cool and dry on the ironing board. Then use the pattern to recut the pocket piece.

Bias pockets are best interfaced with lightweight, fusible interfacing to prevent additional stretching. Cut interfacing on the straight grain to add more stability to your pocket.

To change the look of your garment, cut patch pockets on the bias. (Photo by Jack Deutsch.)

Stretch the fabric as much as you can before cutting out the pocket.

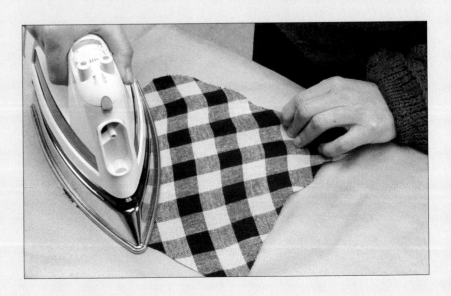

PATCH POCKETS IN SHEER FABRICS

Making a patch pocket in a sheer fabric is a challenge every sewer should accept at some time. Knowing that every seam allowance will show, you must fashion a patch that matches the elegance of the garment. The key is to make a self-lined pocket.

The key to making a patch pocket in a sheer fabric so the seam allowances don't show is to make it self-lined. (Photo by Jack Deutsch.)

Sew a sheer fabric with a 60/8 H needle and fine cotton or rayon thread. Use a sole plate with a hole or your machine's all-purpose sole plate with a piece of tape placed over the opening, to prevent the fragile fabric from being pulled into the machine.

1. To make the pattern piece, cut away the foldback facing from a patch-pocket pattern and place this edge (the pocket top) on a folded piece of paper. Cut around the original pattern piece to make a new, double-sized pattern piece. Cut from fashion fabric and mark the pocket top by making small snips at each end of the paper's foldline.

2. With right sides together, fold the double pocket piece in half at the snip marks. Pin the side and bottom edges together.

3. Using two rows of narrow (0.5 width) zigzag stitches, ⅛ in. apart, sew down each side from the pocket top toward the center of the pocket bottom, leaving an opening of 1½ in. at the bottom. Sewing each side from the top will prevent distortion. Press flat.

4. Trim the seam allowances close to the parallel rows of stitching, keeping the trimmed edge even all the way around, even in the unstitched area. Turn the pocket right side out through the opening in the bottom, using a point turner to push the corners out (see the drawing on the facing page). Press.

5. Following steps 6 and 7 for the unlined patch pocket (see pp. 8-9), position and edgestitch or topstitch your pocket in place, reinforcing the top corners.

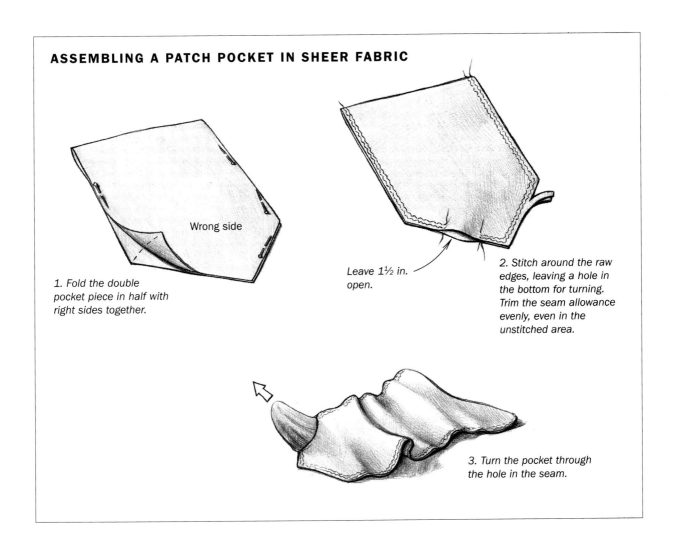

1. Fold the double pocket piece in half with right sides together.

Wrong side

Leave 1½ in. open.

2. Stitch around the raw edges, leaving a hole in the bottom for turning. Trim the seam allowance evenly, even in the unstitched area.

3. Turn the pocket through the hole in the seam.

Patch Pockets with Foldover Flaps

An interesting detail on a patch pocket is the foldover flap. This type of pocket lends itself to all sorts of creative finishes, including piped or corded edges, mock button closures, and fringed edges.

When you add details such as flaps and cording, especially if you're using hand-woven fabrics, it's important to remember that you also add thickness to the finished pocket. To accommodate the thicker layers when sewing the pocket to the garment, change to a heavier needle and lengthen your stitch.

Construction varies with the type of pocket, so let's consider several styles. The simplest is the large rectangular pocket with the top 2½ in. flipped toward the front. The pocket and flap can be self-lined, or the pocket can be lined and the flap faced with fashion fabric.

SELF-LINED PATCH POCKET AND FLAP

1. To make the pocket pattern, cut away the foldback facing from a patch-pocket pattern. Add 2½ in. to this edge (the pocket top) to form the flap. Place the edge of the flap on a folded piece of paper. Cut around the extended pattern piece to make a new, double-sized pattern piece. Cut from fashion fabric, marking the flap edge by making small snips at each end of the paper's foldline, and marking the pocket top (2½ in. from the flap edge) on each side of the double patch with similar snips.

2. Construct the self-lined pocket from the double-sized patch, following steps 2 through 4 for patch pockets in sheer fabrics (see p. 14).

3. Slipstitch by hand on the underside of the fold along the pocket top or machine-stitch through all layers to keep the flap in place. Press the flap toward the front of the pocket.

4. Following steps 6 and 7 for the unlined patch pocket (see pp. 8-9), position and edgestitch or topstitch the pocket to your garment only as far as the foldline, reinforcing the top of the pocket under the fold.

LINED PATCH POCKET WITH SELF-FACED FLAP

1. To make the pocket pattern, cut away the foldback facing from a patch-pocket pattern and add a ⅝-in. seam allowance to this edge (the pocket top). To make the pattern for a 2½-in. flap, cut a piece of paper the width of the pocket piece by a length of 6¼ in. (5 in. plus two seam allowances).

2. Cut the pocket piece from fashion fabric and the lining piece from a lighter fabric. Cut the flap piece from fashion fabric. Fold the flap piece in half widthwise, and mark the foldline with small snips at each end.

3. With right sides together, stitch one edge of the flap piece to the top of the pocket piece, and stitch the other edge of the flap piece to the top of the lining piece (see the drawing on the facing page). Open the pieces out and press the seam allowances toward the flap piece.

4. With right sides together, fold the composite piece in half at the snip marks. Match and pin the side and bottom edges. Stitch around the three edges, leaving an opening of 1½ in. to 2 in. at the bottom.

5. Trim the seam allowances close to the stitching. Turn the pocket and flap right side out through the hole in the bottom, using a point turner to push the corners out. Press.

6. Stitch in the ditch where the flap meets the pocket, to keep the flap in place. Press the flap toward the outside of the pocket.

7. Following steps 6 and 7 for the unlined patch pocket (see pp. 8-9), position and stitch the pocket to your garment only as far as the foldline, reinforcing the top of the pocket under the fold.

ASSEMBLING A PATCH POCKET WITH A FOLDOVER FLAP

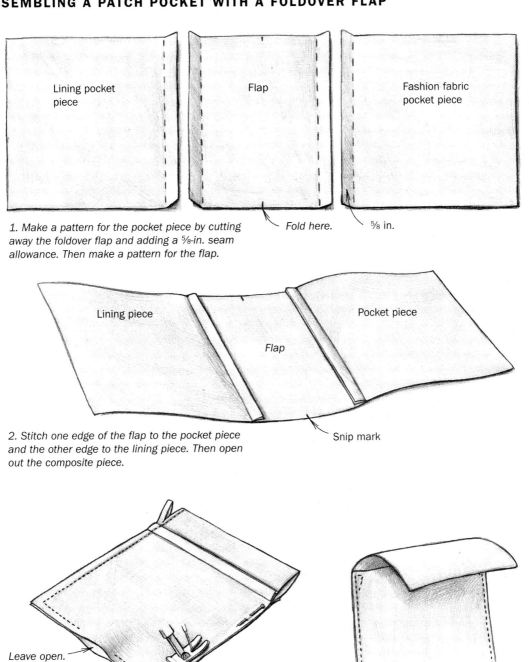

Lining pocket piece

Flap

Fashion fabric pocket piece

Fold here.

⅝ in.

1. Make a pattern for the pocket piece by cutting away the foldover flap and adding a ⅝-in. seam allowance. Then make a pattern for the flap.

Lining piece

Flap

Pocket piece

Snip mark

2. Stitch one edge of the flap to the pocket piece and the other edge to the lining piece. Then open out the composite piece.

Leave open.

3. Fold the composite piece at the snip marks, pin the sides and bottom, and stitch, leaving an opening at the bottom.

4. After stitching in the ditch, press the flap toward the outside of the pocket. When stitching to the garment, stitch only as far as the foldline.

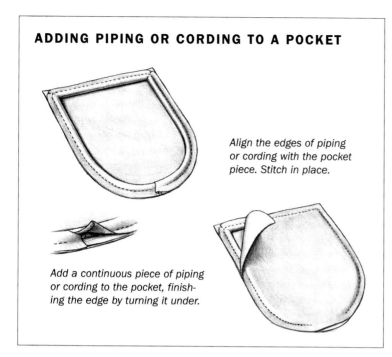

ADDING PIPING OR CORDING TO A POCKET

Align the edges of piping or cording with the pocket piece. Stitch in place.

Add a continuous piece of piping or cording to the pocket, finishing the edge by turning it under.

PIPED OR CORDED PATCH POCKET

Piping or cording is a nice detail on a pocket. You can place it along the top of a lined patch pocket, along the pocket sides and bottom, or along the top of a foldover flap. Purchase or construct the piping as instructed on p. 54.

1. Baste the piping to the edge(s) of the pocket and/or flap piece(s) with a zipper foot, matching the seam allowances. If you are adding piping to the entire patch, the piping should be a continuous piece with no unfinished edges (see the drawing at left). If you are piping the top edge only, or the curved edges only, the raw edges of the piping will be finished when you attach the lining.

2. Construct the pocket as a fully lined patch. Attach the pocket to the garment, using a heavy needle and a long stitch to accommodate the thickness.

FRINGED PATCH POCKET

You can incorporate fringe into your pocket design in two ways. One is by treating it like piping and adding it to the top of a lined patch pocket. Or use a piece of lightweight fringed fabric to make a fully lined patch pocket.

1. Trim away the foldback facing on a patch-pocket pattern. Fold the fringed edge of the fabric to the right side by about 2½ in. Place the top of the pocket pattern (the edge you just cut) along the fabric fold. Cut out the pocket piece (see the drawing on the facing page). Add a ⅝-in. seam allowance to the top of the pocket pattern before cutting out the lining piece.

2. If the fashion fabric is lightweight, stabilize the wrong side as far as the foldline with interfacing and the inside of the foldline with stay tape. If using hand-woven fabric, fuse a strip of interfacing to the wrong side of the flap.

3. Press the seam allowance at the top of the lining piece to the wrong side.

Incorporate the fringed edge of fabric into your design by folding the fringe to the right side and cutting the pocket piece from the folded pocket. (Photo by Jack Deutsch.)

MAKING A PATCH POCKET FROM FRINGED FABRIC

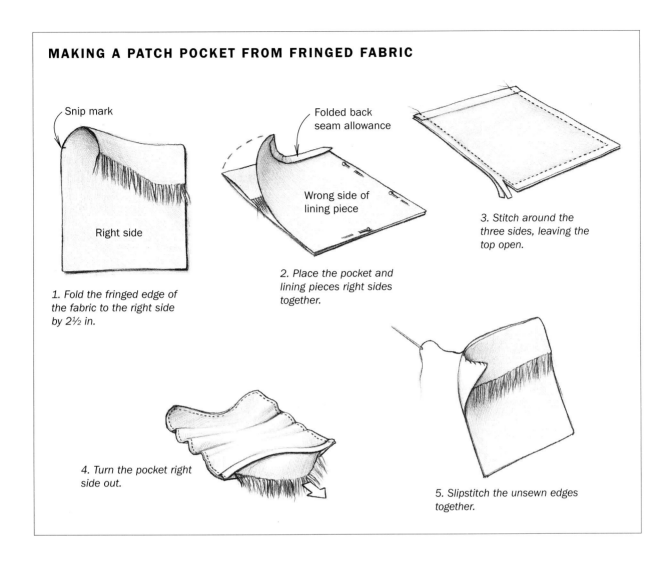

Snip mark

Right side

1. Fold the fringed edge of the fabric to the right side by 2½ in.

Folded back seam allowance

Wrong side of lining piece

2. Place the pocket and lining pieces right sides together.

3. Stitch around the three sides, leaving the top open.

4. Turn the pocket right side out.

5. Slipstitch the unsewn edges together.

Trim ⅟₁₆ in. from the sides and bottom of the lining piece. Making the lining piece a bit smaller than the pocket piece prevents the lining from showing when the pocket is assembled.

4. With right sides together, place the pocket piece against the lining piece, matching the top of the fringed flap to the pressed-back seam allowance. Match and pin the remaining edges.

5. Stitch around the three sides. Remember, because you have trimmed the lining piece, it is slightly smaller than the pocket piece, but you must still match the edges as you sew. Work with

the pocket side down—the feed dogs will help ease the pieces together.

6. Trim the seam allowances close to the stitching. Turn the pocket right side out, using a point turner to push the corners out. Press.

7. Slipstitch the unsewn edge of the lining to the pocket top, close to the foldline.

8. Position and edgestitch the pocket to the garment, anchoring the corners with triangles or double stitching. If the fringed edge has added thickness to the pocket, use a heavier needle and a longer stitch.

Patch Pockets with Buttons and Buttonholes

When should you decide whether or not to add a button and buttonhole to your patch pocket? Before constructing the pocket. The areas under the button and buttonhole need to be interfaced, and this is best done while the fabric pieces are flat (see the drawing below).

Mock button closure

I like the look of a button simply sewn on top of a buttonhole. On a patch pocket, this detail requires only a bit of planning. You decide where the buttonhole will be—perhaps holding a foldover flap in place or as extra embellishment on a patch pocket with decorative braid—and interface the wrong side of the fabric in that area before constructing the pocket.

Fuse an oval of interfacing to the wrong side of the pocket piece where it will be hidden by the foldback facing or the lining (depending on the type of pocket you're making). Complete the pocket and work the buttonhole on the constructed pocket but don't cut it open. Then attach the pocket to the garment.

A mock button closure doesn't have to include a buttonhole. If the button is large or heavy, however, or if the fabric is lightweight or loosely woven, stabilize the fabric with an oval of interfacing fused to the wrong side, under the lining or in the foldback facing (again, depending on the type of pocket you're making). Construct the pocket, then add the button.

Working buttonhole

With not much more planning, you can have a working buttonhole in a patch pocket. On a fully lined patch pocket or on a lined patch pocket with foldback facing, the buttonhole is worked in the pocket and the button is sewn to the garment behind it.

The instructions are much the same as with a mock button closure. Decide where you want the buttonhole, and fuse interfacing to the wrong side of the fabric in that area so it will be hidden by the foldback facing or the lining. Construct the pocket, make the buttonhole, cut it open, and attach the pocket to the garment.

There are great buttons out there just waiting to embellish your garments. Even plain patch pockets—with buttonholes or without—are great places to put them.

MAKING BUTTONHOLES IN PATCH POCKETS

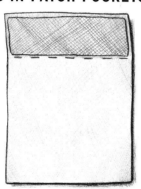

UNLINED PATCH WITH BUTTONHOLE
Fuse interfacing to the wrong side of the pocket piece in the foldback area.

LINED PATCH WITH BUTTONHOLE
Fuse an oval of interfacing to the wrong side of the pocket piece where the buttonhole will be worked...

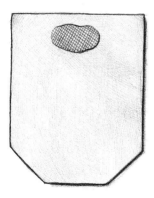

...or fuse interfacing to the wrong side of the entire top of the pocket piece—or even to the entire pocket.

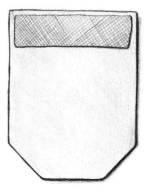

Designer Patch Pockets

Once you have the basic patch-pocket construction techniques down pat, you can start changing pocket size, shape, and details to create your own designer look.

LARGER OR SMALLER PATCH POCKET

One of the easiest changes is to simply make a larger or smaller pocket. Cut paper to the size you want the finished pocket to be, and place it on the garment pattern to see what looks good. Be inventive. Instead of one large patch pocket on each side of your garment, stack two together—a smaller one just above and behind a larger one—or place one pocket on one side of the garment and two on the other side.

If you are petite and always downsize your patterns, beware of downsizing the pocket too much. Make the pocket both narrower and shorter, so its proportions remain the same.

PLEATED OR TUCKED PATCH POCKET

Pocket pleats and tucks come and go with fashion trends. Pleating variations are as endless as your imagination. Most often seen is the patch pocket with a single, inverted box pleat—a military or safari look that's often combined with a flap.

1. Cut the pocket piece the width of the finished pocket plus seam allowances plus twice the width of the finished pleat. For a 2-in. pleat, for example, cut the pocket piece the width of the pocket plus seam allowances plus 4 in.

2. With right sides together, fold the pocket piece in half lengthwise. Stitch just the top inch and the bottom inch, parallel to the folded edge and as far away as the width of the finished pleat (2 in. away in our example). Press the folded edge to define the center of the pleat.

3. From the wrong side of the pocket, flatten and press the pleat in place, matching the center of the pleat with the line created by your stitching. Baste across the ends of the pleat (see the drawing above).

4. For a smooth interior with no lint-catching corners, finish constructing this as a fully lined patch pocket.

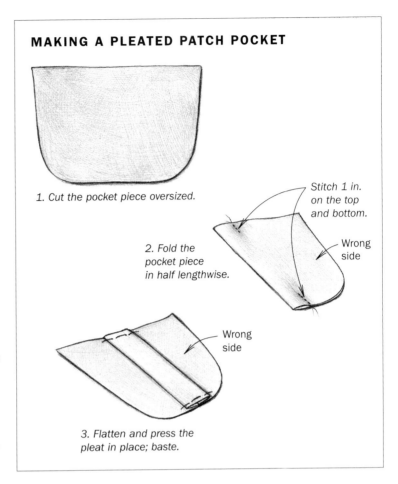

MAKING A PLEATED PATCH POCKET

1. Cut the pocket piece oversized.

2. Fold the pocket piece in half lengthwise.

Stitch 1 in. on the top and bottom.

Wrong side

Wrong side

3. Flatten and press the pleat in place; baste.

PATCH POCKET
WITH CORNER DETAIL

A great designer detail is small rectangles (or other shapes) of fabric stitched over the corners of the pocket opening on the right side of the garment. This is especially interesting on a rotated pocket or on one that opens at the side.

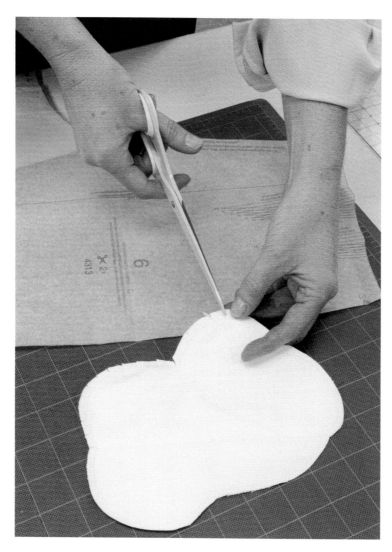

Snip the seam allowances at all the curves and pivot points.

SHAPED PATCH POCKET

It's easy to change the shape of a patch pocket. You can trim away a large part of one corner or round one bottom corner and square the other. You can be whimsical, making a pocket shaped like an apple, an orange, a frog, or a cloud—let your imagination run wild. You can be artistic, even couture, incorporating curves and lines found elsewhere on the garment into the pocket shape or designing a fabulously shaped pocket for an otherwise basic garment. Vintage and designer garments are good sources of inspiration.

It's best to fully line a shaped patch, but the construction technique differs slightly from that of the rectangular lined patch. Let's consider the cloud shape. It has lots of curves, which will look best if the seam allowances are clipped to the stitching line before the pocket is turned.

1. Cut a pocket piece on the straight grain and a lining piece on the bias. If the fashion fabric is light enough, cut the lining piece from it. If you have cut $5/8$-in. seam allowances, trim them to $1/4$ in. On the lining piece, trim away another $1/16$ in.

2. With right sides together and using short stitches, sew the pocket piece to the lining piece $1/4$ in. from the edges all the way around. Snip to but not through the curves and pivot points. Don't cut Vs—make straight cuts (see the photo at left).

3. Make a 2-in. slash in the lining piece (it's the smaller one), somewhere below the center, and turn the pocket through the slash. Finger-press the shaped edges into place, using a point turner to get neat corners and edges. Press.

4. Slip a bit of fusible interfacing under the slash, resin side up. Carefully butt the edges of the slash and fuse together. If you prefer, you can whipstitch the edges closed.

5. If the cloud-shaped pocket is for your toddler's summer outfit, topstitch it to the garment close to the pocket edge. If your shaped pocket is for your inspired-by-a-famous-French-designer jacket, you may want to hand-stitch the pocket to the garment. But first you must baste the pocket securely into position with silk thread. Your basting will become the guideline for your hand stitching.

6. To apply the pocket by hand, work from the wrong side of the garment. Run doubled silk thread through beeswax for strength, and take small, diagonal stitches. Do not take deep stitches that will show on the right side of the garment, and do not pull the stitches too tight. As always, anchor the pocket opening by stitching in from the corners.

PATCH POCKET
WITH TOP CONTRAST

Some of my favorite designer pockets feature top-of-pocket details. One was made popular where I live and teach by teacher/designer Shermane Fouché. She constructed her popular silk-charmeuse blouse with the shiny side in, but the tops of the unlined patch pockets had shiny self-facings. The idea was to con-trast the interesting wrong side of the fabric against the right side.

1. Fold the wrong side of the pocket top to the right side of the pocket by ½ in., then fold again by another ½ in. Press.

2. Topstitch close to the folded hem edge (see the drawing below). Press.

3. Following steps 4 through 8 for the unlined patch pocket (see the pp. 4-9), but eliminating the turn in step 5, complete and stitch the pocket to your garment.

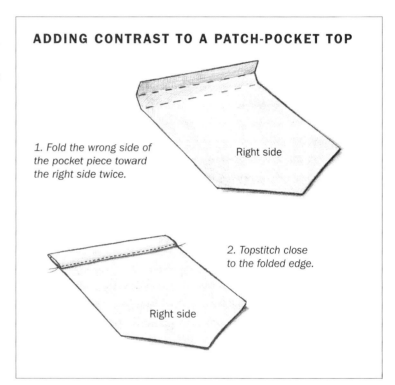

ADDING CONTRAST TO A PATCH-POCKET TOP

1. Fold the wrong side of the pocket piece toward the right side twice.

Right side

2. Topstitch close to the folded edge.

Right side

PATCH POCKET WITH TOP BANDING: METHOD 1

Banding a lined pocket provides interesting top-of-pocket detail. The banding can contrast in color or in grain line. You can add detail to the banding, or pleat or gather the pocket into it.

The simplest way to band a pocket is by stitching a folded piece of fabric to both the pocket and the lining.

1. Cut a piece of fabric the width of the pocket piece and twice the depth of the finished banding plus seam allowances.

2. With right sides together, stitch one long edge of the banding to the top of the pocket piece. If your banding is very narrow, use a ¼-in. seam allowance; otherwise, a ⅝-in. seam allowance is fine. Press the seam allowance open. If you're using a sheer fabric or a color that will show through on the pocket, press the seam allowance toward the banding.

3. With right sides together and using the same seam allowance as before, stitch the other long edge of the banding to the top of the lining piece (see the drawing below). Press the seam allowance as you did on the pocket piece. If the fabric is bulky, grade the seam allowances.

4. Following steps 4 through 7 for the lined patch pocket with self-faced flap (see p. 16), complete and stitch the pocket to your garment.

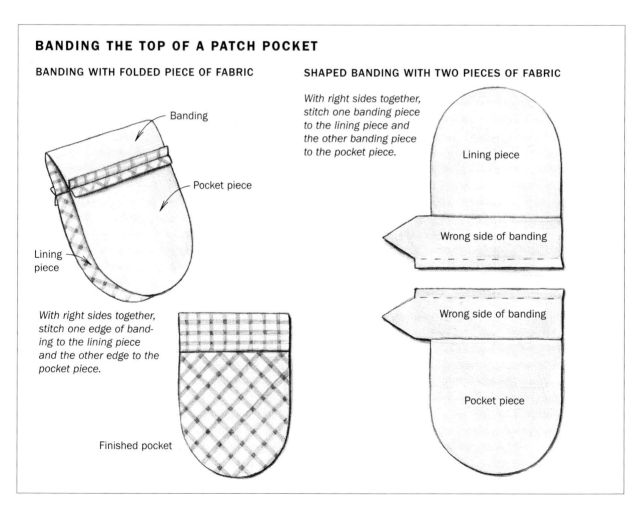

BANDING THE TOP OF A PATCH POCKET

BANDING WITH FOLDED PIECE OF FABRIC

Banding

Pocket piece

Lining piece

With right sides together, stitch one edge of banding to the lining piece and the other edge to the pocket piece.

Finished pocket

SHAPED BANDING WITH TWO PIECES OF FABRIC

With right sides together, stitch one banding piece to the lining piece and the other banding piece to the pocket piece.

Lining piece

Wrong side of banding

Wrong side of banding

Pocket piece

24

PATCH POCKET WITH TOP BANDING: METHOD 2

If you wish to shape the banding or the pocket, you'll need to use two banding pieces instead of one. One will be stitched to the pocket piece and the other to the lining piece.

1. Cut two banding pieces the depth of the finished banding plus seam allowances.

2. With right sides together, stitch one long edge of one banding piece to the pocket piece. Use a ¼-in. seam allowance if your banding is very narrow or a ⅝-in. seam allowance if the banding is wider. Press the seam allowance toward the banding.

3. With right sides together and using the same seam allowance as before, stitch one long edge of the other banding piece to the lining piece, but leave an opening of 1½ in. Press as you did on the pocket piece.

4. Join the banding pieces along the unsewn edges. Clip curves and snip into points, if any. Press the seam allowances toward the banding.

5. Construct the pocket as usual, following steps 1 through 5 for the fully lined patch pocket (see pp. 10-11), but turning the pocket through the opening where the banding meets the lining instead of at the bottom of the pocket.

PATCH POCKET WITH DECORATIVE BRAID

Decorative braid is one of the most-recognized designer pocket details (see the photo above). Purchase enough woven braid to go across the top of all

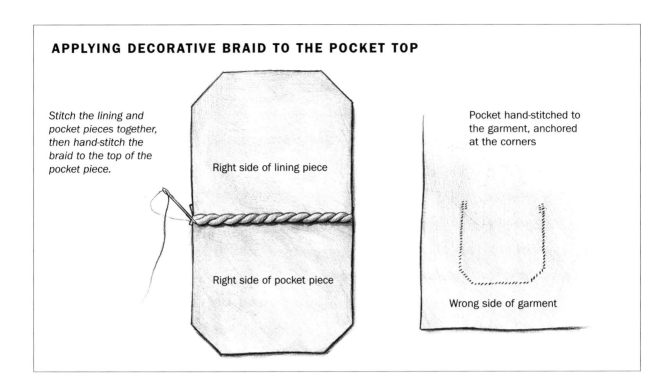

APPLYING DECORATIVE BRAID TO THE POCKET TOP

Stitch the lining and pocket pieces together, then hand-stitch the braid to the top of the pocket piece.

Right side of lining piece

Right side of pocket piece

Pocket hand-stitched to the garment, anchored at the corners

Wrong side of garment

the pockets on the garment front, including seam allowances. Since this is a couture look, hand-stitch the pockets to the garment.

1. Trim $\frac{1}{16}$ in. from the sides and bottom of the lining piece. Don't trim the top. Making the lining piece a bit smaller than the pocket piece prevents the lining from showing when the pocket is assembled.

2. With right sides together, stitch the lining piece to the pocket piece along the top edge. Press. Trim the seam allowance to $\frac{1}{4}$ in.

3. On the right side of the composite piece, hand-sew the braid to the top of the pocket piece without catching the lining piece. This ensures that the braid will be right at the top edge of the finished pocket.

4. Following steps 3 through 5 for the fully lined patch pocket (see pp. 10-11), complete and hand-sew the pocket to your garment, referring to step 6 on p. 23 and the drawing above.

PATCH POCKET
WITH ELASTIC-FILLED CASING

A short designer rain jacket I saw in a small boutique featured patch pockets topped with elastic-filled casings. The elastic was not especially taut and the pockets did not appear gathered; they looked like perfectly shaped patches. The pockets were cut larger at the tops and pulled back into place with the elastic.

1. Trim away the foldback facing from the top of a patch-pocket pattern. Draw two vertical lines on the pocket pattern,

ADDING ELASTIC TO THE POCKET TOP

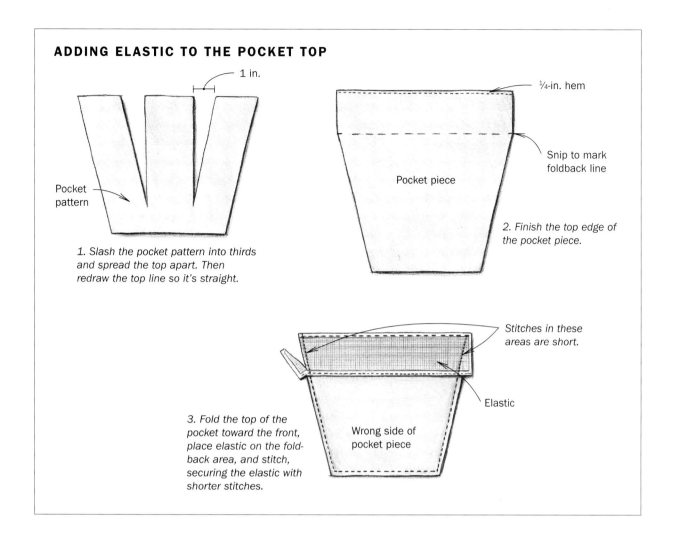

1 in.

Pocket pattern

1. Slash the pocket pattern into thirds and spread the top apart. Then redraw the top line so it's straight.

¼-in. hem

Pocket piece

Snip to mark foldback line

2. Finish the top edge of the pocket piece.

Stitches in these areas are short.

Elastic

3. Fold the top of the pocket toward the front, place elastic on the fold-back area, and stitch, securing the elastic with shorter stitches.

Wrong side of pocket piece

---

dividing it into thirds. Slash almost to the bottom of each line and spread the top of each slash apart by about 1 in. Redraw the top line so it's straight. Add a new foldback facing, as wide as the redrafted pocket and deep enough to accommodate a wide piece of elastic plus the edge finish.

2. After cutting the piece out of fabric, mark the foldback line at the top of the pocket piece by making a small snip at each end.

3. Finish the top edge of the pocket piece with an overlock stitch or with a ¼-in. hem.

4. With the pocket piece right side up, fold and press the top of the pocket toward the front along the foldback line. Measure the fold to be sure it's even all the way across. Pin or baste the foldback.

5. Cut a piece of elastic as long as the *original* pattern piece was wide. Pin the ends to each edge of the foldback area. The elastic is on top of your work.

6. Stitch around the sides and bottom of the pocket, shortening the stitches in the foldback area and catching the elastic in the stitching (see the drawing on p. 27).

7. Trim the seam allowances (fabric and elastic) in the foldback area. Turn the foldback to the wrong side of the pocket. Press.

8. Finish the casing by topstitching across the bottom of the foldback facing. Press.

9. Press all edges of the pocket to the wrong side along the stitching lines. Position and edgestitch the pocket to your garment.

GATHERED PATCH POCKET

A friend's *très chic* dress features softly gathered, gently drooping pockets anchored in vertical seams near the hem. To make this type of pocket you must reshape the pattern piece.

CREATING A SOFTLY DROOPING POCKET

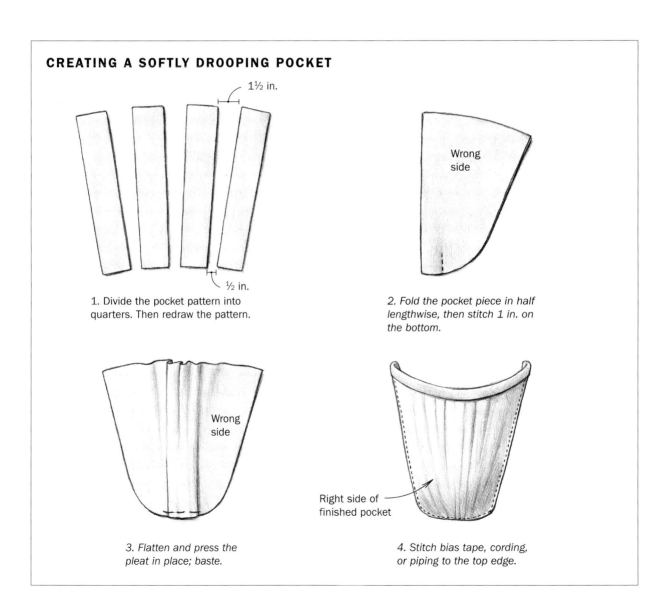

1½ in.

½ in.

1. Divide the pocket pattern into quarters. Then redraw the pattern.

Wrong side

2. Fold the pocket piece in half lengthwise, then stitch 1 in. on the bottom.

Wrong side

3. Flatten and press the pleat in place; baste.

Right side of finished pocket

4. Stitch bias tape, cording, or piping to the top edge.

1. Draw three vertical lines on the pocket pattern, dividing it into quarters. Cut the pattern apart along the lines. Spread the top of the pocket by about 1½ in. at each slash, and the bottom by ½ in. at each slash (see the drawing on the facing page). Redraw the pocket.

2. After cutting the piece out of fabric, fold the pocket piece in half lengthwise with right sides together. Stitch just the bottom inch, parallel to and ¾ in. from the folded edge to form an inverted pleat. Press the folded edge to define the center of the pleat.

3. From the wrong side of the pocket, flatten and press the pleat into place, matching the center of the pleat with the line created by your stitching. Baste across the end of the pleat.

4. Gather the top edge of the pocket so it's wider than the original pattern piece by 1 in. or 2 in.

5. With right sides together and aligning raw edges, stitch self-fabric bias tape, piping, or cording to the top edge of the pocket. Press the seam allowance toward the pocket. If you're using bias tape, press the raw edge under on the inside of the pocket. Stitch in the ditch from the right side to secure.

6. Finish the bottom edge of the pocket by pressing ⅝ in. to the wrong side and edgestitching the bottom of the pocket to your garment, catching the sides of the pocket in the vertical seams in the garment.

7. Alternatively, finish the pocket as an unlined patch. Stay-stitch around the unfinished curved edges of the pocket, then press them to the wrong side. Trim cording, if you have added it, so there is no cording in the seam allowances. Topstitch the pocket in place on your garment, then turn the pocket inside out and *carefully* trim the seam allowance.

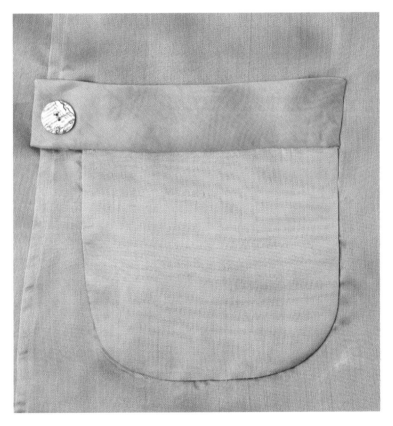

A patch pocket doesn't have to be basic. It can be a fabulous addition to any garment, simple or couture. (Photo by Jack Deutsch.)

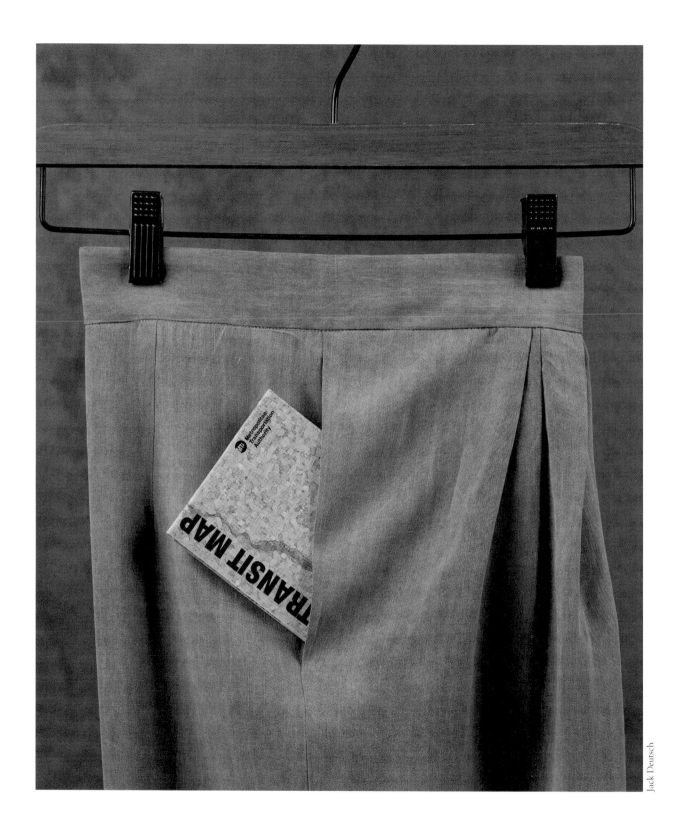

IN-SEAM POCKETS

In-seam pockets are the most utilitarian of pockets. These are the pockets where you stash your cash before slipping out of the office for a midafternoon cappuccino, where you put your house key while walking the dog, or where you stuff your hands while trying to look nonchalant. Most important, these are pockets that blend in with the garment, so there is more forgiveness in the sewing process.

The two most common types of in-seam pockets are side seam and slant front. Both have variations: A side-seam pocket can be placed in any seam, horizontal or vertical, and a slant-front pocket can conceal a waistband opening.

SIDE-SEAM POCKETS

There are several types of side-seam pockets (see the drawing below). The first is constructed by sewing one pocket piece to the garment front and one pocket piece to the garment back, then sewing the front and back garment pieces and pocket pieces together as a unit. This is known as the basic side-seam pocket. Three other types include a faced side-seam pocket, characterized by part of the pocket bag being constructed with fashion fabric and the remainder with pocketing or lining material; a side-seam pocket with pocket extensions, which has the finished look of the faced side-seam pocket; and a cut-on pocket, where the garment front and garment back pieces are cut to include the pocket pieces.

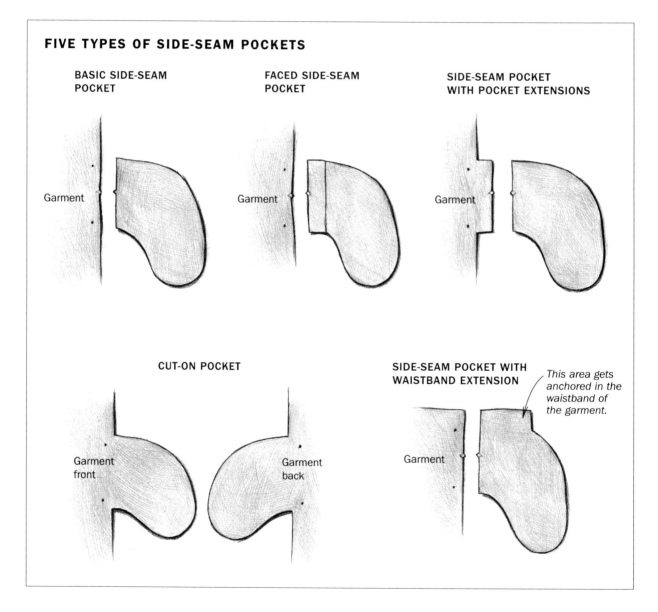

FIVE TYPES OF SIDE-SEAM POCKETS

BASIC SIDE-SEAM POCKET

Garment

FACED SIDE-SEAM POCKET

Garment

SIDE-SEAM POCKET WITH POCKET EXTENSIONS

Garment

CUT-ON POCKET

Garment front

Garment back

SIDE-SEAM POCKET WITH WAISTBAND EXTENSION

This area gets anchored in the waistband of the garment.

Garment

Create Your Own Side-Seam Pocket

As the sewer of the fabulous garment you are working on, you are the one who gets to choose the design details. This includes the pocket design. Just because the pattern illustration shows patch or welt pockets doesn't mean that you have to construct patch or welt pockets. It is quite easy to substitute a side-seam pocket for any pocket design.

Start by borrowing a shaped side-seam pocket piece from another pattern (or just use the rectangular patch pocket piece). Cut out four pocket pieces using this pattern. The placement of the side-seam pocket on the garment will be similar to that of the patch pocket, so mark the side garment seams to indicate where the top of the pocket will be, then follow these steps.

1. Pin each pocket piece to the front and back garment pieces, using the markings you have made on the side seams as placement guides.

2. Sew each pocket piece in place using a ⅜-in. seam allowance (see step 4 on p. 37).

3. Press the pocket pieces to the side of the garment.

4. Now place each front garment piece to a back piece with right sides together. Sew the side seams with a ⅝-in. seam allowance. Sew to approximately 1½ in. below the top of the pocket join to the garment. Baste across the pocket opening, then sew again from about 1½ in. above the bottom of the pocket join to the hem of the garment. (The pocket needs to be deeper than the opening so stuff doesn't fall out.)

5. Press the side seams open; clip the back seam allowances above and below the pocket; press the pocket pieces toward the front of the garment.

6. If you want to topstitch the pocket in place, on a jacket for instance, pin, then baste the pocket pieces to the front of the garment. Topstitch the pocket piece in place from the right side using your basting stitches as a guide.

7. Remove the basting stitches from the pocket opening and the top of the garment. Press.

A side-seam pocket with a waistband extension is another version of an in-seam pocket and is found, of course, in pants and skirts, which have waistbands. The pocket pieces in this construction are shaped so that the pocket will be anchored in the waistband of the garment being constructed.

BEFORE YOU SEW

An important thing to remember about side-seam pockets is that they are not going to show on the outside of the garment. Therefore, you can use lining fabric, cotton batiste, or pocketing material for the pocket pieces as easily as you can use fashion fabric. Keep in mind that the basic side-seam pocket and the side-seam pocket with a waistband extension often spread open just enough for you to see the pocket back piece. So you may want to use fashion fabric for at least the pocket back pieces or construct a faced side-seam pocket.

A well-constructed side-seam pocket blends in with the garment and is not bulky, even in this soft silk. This pocket has a waistband extension, is made of fashion fabric, and has no interfacing in the side seams. (Photo by Jack Deutsch.)

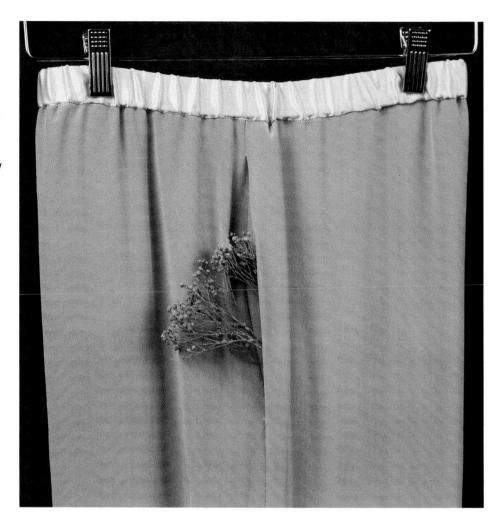

Let's take a moment to talk about the use of lining or pocketing material rather than fashion fabric. Lining fabric is characterized by its "slipperiness" as well as by its being light in weight. My favorite lining fabric is Bemberg rayon. Bemberg comes in two weights and lots of colors (see Resources on p. 101), so I can get a good color match for almost any fabric. Occasionally I will use an acetate lining, which tends to be crisper than rayon, but I never use polyester lining. Polyester doesn't press well and is a difficult fabric to work with; plus it doesn't breathe.

I have a penchant for fine fabrics—wools, silks, linens, and linen-silk-rayon blends fill my fabric coffers, with the occasional velour thrown in. Most of these fabrics are light in weight. I don't want garments made of these fabrics to have bulky or stiff pockets, so I sometimes use fashion fabric for the pocket pieces, or I use a combination of fashion fabric and lining fabric. I get the best results with these options.

Pocketing material is a tight-weave cotton that works well for some pockets. You often see this fabric in the faced side-seam pockets found in men's trousers, and you can copy this when making similar garments—tailored slacks and jacket pockets. Its neutral "natural" color works well with light-color garments. Before using it, though, hold it and the fashion fabric in your hand at the same time. If the pocketing seems too heavy for the fashion fabric but you like the feel of a cotton pocket, use cotton batiste (but not the really light kind) or a piece of good-quality, even-weave, 100% cotton for one or both of the pocket pieces. If you decide to use pocketing, preshrink it first.

MARKING AND INTERFACING

Very few markings are necessary in the construction of side-seam pockets. It is essential to mark the pocket opening on the garment front and back pieces. Also there are "match point'" markings—usually notches—on the garment front and back pieces and on the pocket pieces. Make sure you transfer these markings from the pattern to the fabric pieces, too.

Before you begin constructing the pockets in any garment, you should decide whether or not interfacing is needed. For side-seam pockets, the only place on the garment that might need extra stabilizing or strengthening is along the seam allowance of the garment front where the pocket is located. Get in the habit of thinking about the finished garment: Is the pocket going to add weight to the seam, and what

effect will that weight have? Will the seam become wavy? Will the pocket droop and distort the garment? Will the fabric stretch after the pocket is used a few times?

If you answered yes to one or more of these questions, you should interface the garment front piece in the area of the pocket opening, since the front seam allowance is the part of the pocket that is stressed most when used. Use a $\frac{3}{4}$-in. strip of fusible interfacing that is about 2 in. longer than the pocket opening. Fuse the interfacing on the wrong side of the garment front piece along the seam allowance so that it extends beyond the pocket opening about 1 in. in either direction.

Now that we have discussed interfacing to eliminate potential problems, I must admit that I rarely have experienced problems. Consequently, I rarely interface.

SEWING A BASIC POCKET

This brings us to the actual construction process, which proceeds as follows.

1. After cutting out the pocket pieces and garment pieces, transfer all markings to the fabric, including the notches that mark the pocket placement and the marks or notches that mark the pocket opening. My method for marking is to snip the seam allowances about $\frac{1}{8}$ in. where there are notches or lines and to use tailor tacks where there are dots or small shapes. Other marking devices include chalk or various types of marking pens, but before using any, make sure the marks can be removed from the farbic or be careful to mark the *wrong* side of the fabric.

2. If your fabric requires it, interface the area along the pocket opening of the garment front piece by placing a $\frac{3}{4}$-in. strip of fusible tricot along the seam

CONSTRUCTING A BASIC SIDE-SEAM POCKET

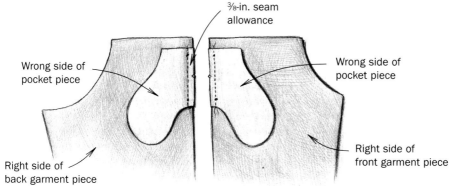

⅜-in. seam allowance

Wrong side of pocket piece

Wrong side of pocket piece

Right side of front garment piece

Right side of back garment piece

1. Attach the pocket pieces to the garment pieces with right sides together.

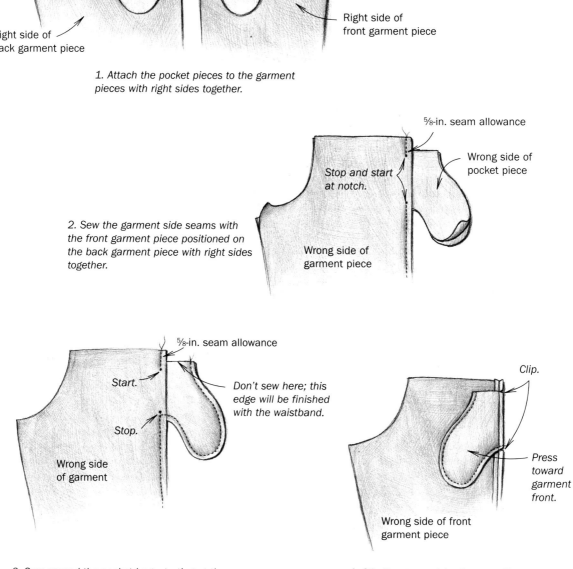

⅝-in. seam allowance

Stop and start at notch.

Wrong side of pocket piece

Wrong side of garment piece

2. Sew the garment side seams with the front garment piece positioned on the back garment piece with right sides together.

⅝-in. seam allowance

Start.

Stop.

Don't sew here; this edge will be finished with the waistband.

Wrong side of garment

3. Sew around the pocket bag, starting at the side seam at the top of the pocket and ending at the bottom of the pocket opening.

Clip.

Press toward garment front.

Wrong side of front garment piece

4. Clip the garment back seam allowances above and below the pocket.

allowance on the wrong side of the garment piece. Extend the interfacing past the pocket opening approximately 1 in. in each direction.

3. With right sides together, position one of the pocket pieces on the front garment piece and the other on the back garment piece. Pin. Hand-baste if you are working with a silk or slippery fabric that might move around under the needle on the sewing machine.

4. Attach the pocket pieces to the garment pieces with a ⅜-in. or ½-in. seam allowance (see the drawing on the facing page). Don't attach the pocket pieces with a ⅝-in. seam allowance. A ⅝-in. seam allowance would be right along the garment side seam, creating bulk where all the seam allowances will be pressed back under the side seam. Using a narrower seam allowance (I've even seen instructions for using a ¼-in. seam allowance) to attach the pockets eliminates the bulk, and the pocket attachment seams won't show on the outside of the garment.

5. Press each pocket piece out, toward the side of the garment.

6. If you intend to topstitch the finished garment, now is the time to topstitch the pocket opening. Sew from the top. (It's called topstitching because you sew from the top, which is the right side of the garment.) Start and stop your topstitching so that it matches the pocket opening. Backstitching at the beginning and end of your topstitching is going to be noticeable, so either pull the thread end to the wrong side or lock the stitch in place by pulling the fabric

as you sew so that the sewing machine sews in one place for a stitch or two— a dressmaker's trick for locking the stitches without building up a lot of thread at the beginning and end of a seam.

7. The next step is to sew the garment side seams. With right sides together, place the garment front with pocket piece against the garment back with pocket piece, matching the top and bottom edge of the garment, the pocket opening markings, and other notches along the seam line. Sew from the top of the garment to the top of the pocket opening (indicated by a tailor tack, snip, or mark), backstitching at the end of your stitching. Sew from the bottom of the pocket opening to the hem or bottom edge of the garment.

8. While the garment pieces are still in position, complete the pocket by sewing around the pocket bag, starting at the side seam at the top of the pocket and continuing all around the curve of the pocket to the bottom of the pocket opening. Don't leave any little holes for your earring to fall through!

9. Clip the seam allowances of the back garment piece so that the pocket can fall toward the front of the garment. Voilà, a basic side-seam pocket.

SEWING A FACED POCKET

The faced side-seam pocket is sewn exactly like the basic side-seam pocket, but first you must sew the facing in place on the pocket back. Don't just overlock the edge of the fashion fabric facing piece then stitch the facing in place through the overlocking onto the lining/pocketing piece. This is a "made at home" look, and you are likely to have little threads in your pockets all the

Finishing the Seams

Consider the following when deciding whether to finish the seams around a side-seam pocket.

These are the seams: the garment side seams and the pocket-piece attachment seams, plus the curve of the pocket, called the pocket bag. These are your options: leaving the seams unfinished, overlocking the seams, sewing a seam finish, and binding the seams. If you combine all the options, there could be an entire chapter on the subject, so let's consider a couple of situations.

If you are whipping up this garment to wear soon—really soon—sew it and wear it and forget about seam finishes. Another option is to overlock everything: overlock each piece before you sew it to any other piece, overlock the seam allowances together after you have attached the pocket pieces, overlock around the pocket pieces—but do clip the seam allowances above and below the pocket first and be very careful not to cut your garment when serging (see the drawing on p. 36). If you are working with a lightweight piece of fabric, remember that when you press the multiple threads of the overlocked area, they may leave an impression on the right side of the fabric.

If you are working with a fabric that ravels easily, you are probably going to want to finish the garment seams to contain the raveling, and if you enjoy the process of creating a garment that looks as good on the in-side as on the outside, you are probably going to want to finish the seams to enhance the garment's look.

One option is to finish all the straight seams and leave the pocket bag unfinished. Fabric has two straight grains: the lengthwise grain and the crosswise grain; bias is the diagonal line that goes between, and we know that bias doesn't ravel, or ravels very little. When you have a curved pattern piece like an in-seam pocket piece, much of the curve is on the bias and won't ravel.

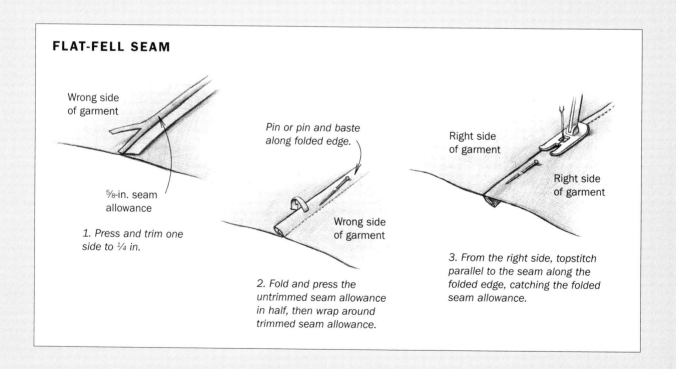

FLAT-FELL SEAM

Wrong side of garment

⅝-in. seam allowance

1. Press and trim one side to ¼ in.

Pin or pin and baste along folded edge.

Wrong side of garment

2. Fold and press the untrimmed seam allowance in half, then wrap around trimmed seam allowance.

Right side of garment

Right side of garment

3. From the right side, topstitch parallel to the seam along the folded edge, catching the folded seam allowance.

Flat-fell seams

A classic, sewn finish that lends itself to the construction of side-seam pockets is the flat-fell seam, especially on the pocket attachment seams of a side-seam pocket with pocket extensions. Even if the rest of the seams in the garment are left unfinished, flat-fell seams on these short seam allowances keep the seam allowances, well, flat. They contain the raw edges, and they look good on both the right side and the wrong side of the fabric. Construct a flat-fell seam as follows.

1. After sewing and pressing the seam allowance, trim one side of the seam allowance by ⅜ in. Press the untrimmed seam allowance over the trimmed seam once, then press in half, tucking the trimmed seam allowance inside. Pin or pin and baste the folded seam allowance along the folded edge.

2. Turn the garment right side up. Topstitch the folded seam allowance in place along the folded edge, following the basting line or the line of pins. The stitching line should be parallel to the seam line.

Mock-fell seams

Another seam finish to consider is mock-fell seams. This seam finish also contains raveling, but takes less time (and a little less skill) to construct than classic flat-fell seams.

Construct a mock-fell seam as follows.

1. After sewing and pressing the seams, trim one side of the seam allowance to ⅜ in. Pink or overlock the untrimmed seam allowance, or leave it unfinished. Press the untrimmed seam allowance flat over the trimmed one and pin or pin and baste onto the garment.

2. Sew the untrimmed seam allowance down, keeping the stitching line parallel to the seam line. The trimmed seam allowance will be hidden by the stitched-down seam allowance. (Because it is easy to keep your stitches parallel to the seam line, it is not necessary to sew from the right side of the garment.)

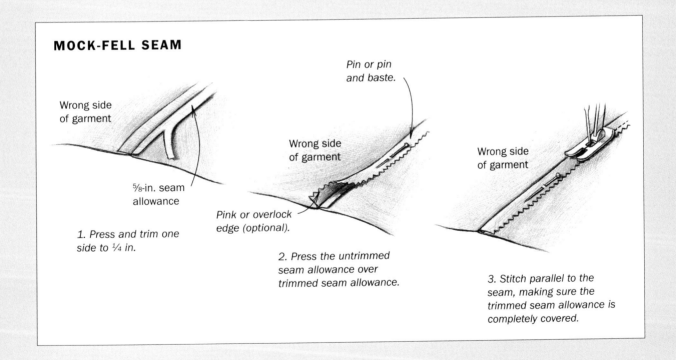

MOCK-FELL SEAM

Wrong side of garment

⅝-in. seam allowance

1. Press and trim one side to ¼ in.

Wrong side of garment

Pink or overlock edge (optional).

2. Press the untrimmed seam allowance over trimmed seam allowance.

Pin or pin and baste.

Wrong side of garment

3. Stitch parallel to the seam, making sure the trimmed seam allowance is completely covered.

Binding the Pocket Bag

Consider binding the curved seam allowances of the pocket bag. These edges are cut cross-grain and won't ravel much under any circumstances, but a gorgeous pair of slinky silk pull-on pants or even a robe that might fall open and reveal its internal construction to the world are garments with seams that are candidates for binding. Here are the steps to follow.

1. Binding a seam requires strips of bias, which you can make yourself with garment fabric or from contrasting fabric. Packaged double-fold bias tape is also an option. Make your own bias by cutting strips 1½ in. wide by however long the pocket bag measures, plus some extra for the beginning and end. Prepare the bias by pressing it in half, and pressing each half in half again.

2. Clip the seam allowances above and below the pocket, then trim the seam allowances you are binding to ¼ in.

3. Sew the bias strip to the trimmed seam allowances, matching the stitching line of the pocket bag with one of the side folds of the bias strip (see the left drawing on the facing page). Leave a 1-in. tail of bias at the beginning. Sew the bias strip all the way around the pocket bag, curving the end up to the bottom of the pocket opening. Leave a tail at this end, too, approximately 1 in. long.

4. For a neat finish, unfold the bias strip at each end and tuck the 1-in. tail in toward the pocket bag. It may be necessary to trim the tail to eliminate bulk.

5. Working on the ironing board, refold and press the bias strip over the pocket bag seam allowances.

Slipstitch or topstitch the bias, binding the seam allowances.

I rarely like to work with bias strips that are less than 1½ in. wide, but I do trim the strip after I have attached it if I think the finished, bound seam will be too wide or wider than I want. You are in charge here, so you can choose.

There is an alternate way of constructing bias-finished seams that requires less fussing. Create the double-fold bias, as described in step 1, but fold both sides in, then simply slip it over the trimmed seam allowances (see the right drawing on the facing page). Sew through all thicknesses.

If you master this binding technique on pockets that don't show, just imagine how you can use it where it does show. Try it!

time. (Have you ever bought a garment that was made like this?) Take the time to seam the facing piece to the lining/pocketing piece with right sides together. You can overlock the edge and press it to one side for a neat finish. Once you have faced the pocket pieces, proceed through the basic side-seam pocket construction (see pp. 35-37). (Usually you only face two of the four pocket pieces, so make sure you attach the two faced pieces to the garment back pieces.)

SEWING A CUT-ON POCKET

The cut-on side-seam pocket is constructed by following the steps to create the basic side-seam pocket (see pp. 35-37), but skip steps 3 and 4.

SEWING A SIDE-SEAM POCKET WITH POCKET EXTENSIONS

The side-seam pocket with pocket extensions is a combination of a cut-on side-seam pocket and a basic side-seam pocket. Part of the pocket is cut on—

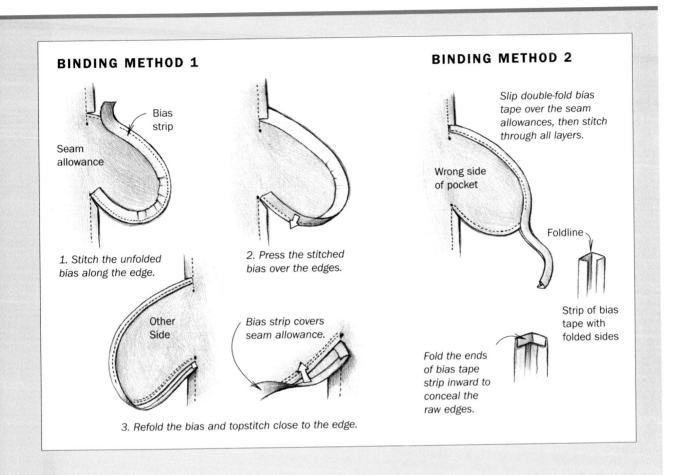

BINDING METHOD 1

Bias strip

Seam allowance

1. Stitch the unfolded bias along the edge.

2. Press the stitched bias over the edges.

Other Side

Bias strip covers seam allowance.

3. Refold the bias and topstitch close to the edge.

BINDING METHOD 2

Slip double-fold bias tape over the seam allowances, then stitch through all layers.

Wrong side of pocket

Foldline

Strip of bias tape with folded sides

Fold the ends of bias tape strip inward to conceal the raw edges.

this is the extension—and the pocket pieces are seamed to the extensions before the pocket is completed as a basic version. When completing the pocket bag, be careful to start right at the side seam, not at the seam of the extension.

You may find that the pocket opening mark is not where you start stitching around the pocket bag, but is down an inch or so. This is true of most side-seam pockets. The things you put in your pocket will stay there if the pocket opening is smaller than the pocket, and the pocket will hang nicely and not distort the side seam.

SEWING A SIDE-SEAM POCKET WITH WAISTBAND EXTENSION

The side-seam pocket with a waistband extension is virtually the same as the basic side-seam pocket, except that the top of the pocket is not sewn shut when you complete the pocket bag. This part will be closed when the waistband is attached.

Creating a Pocket under the Side Seam

Pull-on pants were never the same after Marcy Tilton, founder of The Sewing Workshop, popularized a simple-to-make but different pocket—the pocket centered under the side seam. This pocket is constructed by centering, then attaching a pocket piece under the side seam.

1. After cutting out the pattern pieces, cut a large rectangle that is 8 in. wide and 14 in. long. Cut a V-shape on one of the short sides. This will be the bottom of the pocket. Overlock the edges of all pieces for a neat and easy finish.

2. Begin constructing the pocket by completing the side seam in the garment up to a point 6 in. to 7 in. from the waistline edge. Sew the side seam 1 in. down from the waistline edge. Press the seams open.

3. Cut ½-in. by 9-in. strips of double-face fusible interfacing (Stitch

This pocket centered under the side seam is enhanced by the stitching outlining the pocket piece. (Photo by Jack Deutsch.)

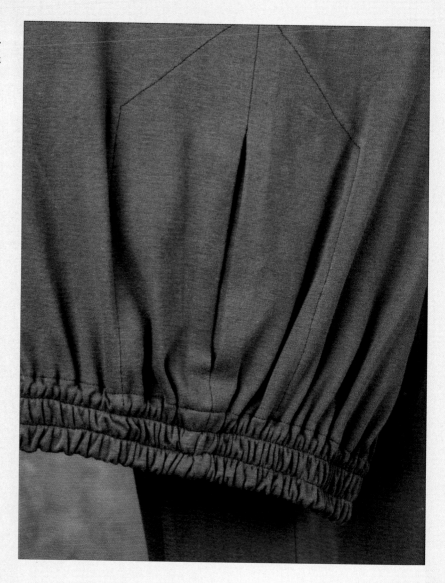

Witchery, for example) and slip one under each seam allow-ance. Fuse the seam allowances in place to prevent the pocket opening from stretching out of shape. Topstitch along each side of the pocket opening now, if you choose.

4. On the wrong side of the fabric, center the pocket piece over the seam, matching the unshaped edge with the waistline edge of the pants. Pin or pin and baste the pocket piece in place.

5. From the right side of the garment, topstitch the pocket in place, using the pins or basting line as a guide. Remove the pins or basting and press.

6. Anchor the top of the pocket in the waistband of the garment.

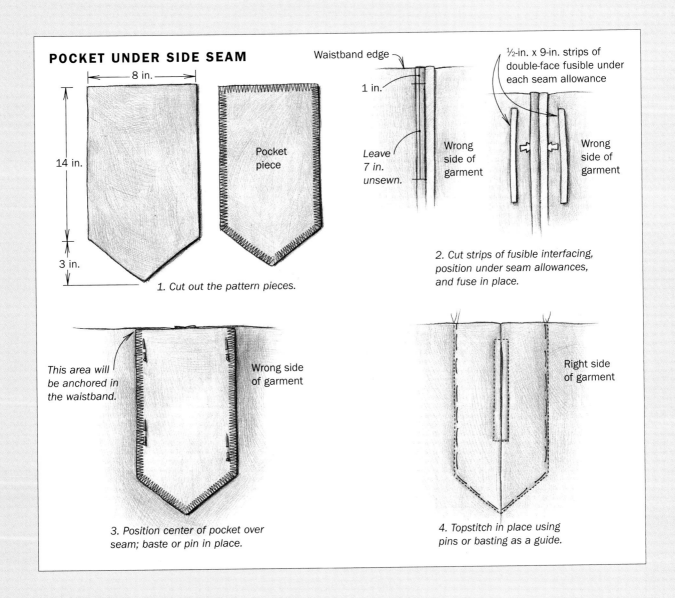

POCKET UNDER SIDE SEAM

8 in.

14 in.

3 in.

Pocket piece

1. Cut out the pattern pieces.

Waistband edge

1 in.

Leave 7 in. unsewn.

Wrong side of garment

½-in. x 9-in. strips of double-face fusible under each seam allowance

Wrong side of garment

2. Cut strips of fusible interfacing, position under seam allowances, and fuse in place.

This area will be anchored in the waistband.

Wrong side of garment

3. Position center of pocket over seam; baste or pin in place.

Right side of garment

4. Topstitch in place using pins or basting as a guide.

SLANT-FRONT POCKETS

Slightly more difficult to construct than side-seam pockets are slant-front pockets, which are often called hip-front, U-shape, or western pockets. These are basically all variations on a theme. The garment front has a cut shape—diagonal is the most common; the U-shape is typical of jeans or western wear; some garments sport squared-off openings.

The pocket is constructed by combining the shaped garment front, a pocket underlay most often cut from lining or pocketing material rather than from fashion fabric, and the garment side front, which is partly visible from the front of the garment and partly becomes the pocket back.

BEFORE YOU SEW

Waist and hip alterations are made in all three pieces before you cut the pattern. After you have altered and cut out the pieces, transfer all markings from the paper pattern to the fabric. Darts, notches, and square corners all need to be marked. It is important to remember that some of these pockets span the hip bones, and some are designed to stand away from the body more than the amount necessary to accommodate your body's curves. The match points will help you get the shape your pattern dictates.

Before you start to sew, have a length of linen stay tape or rayon seam binding on hand to use along the pocket edge. The linen stay tape will prevent the pocket opening from stretching and sagging. As an alternative to linen stay tape, the selvage of a piece of lining fabric will also work—especially great for color coordination!

You may want to consider interfacing the side seam allowance on the garment back piece where it connects to the lower part of the finished pocket. This is the area where the three joined pocket pieces are sewn to the garment back. This seam can sometimes look wavy in this area because the combined weight of the front and pocket pieces is greater than the weight of the garment back in the seam-allowance area. A strip of $\frac{3}{4}$-in.-wide fusible interfacing extending from the pocket opening down about 4 in. will do the trick.

This slant-front pocket has the classic diagonal line, which is topstitched here. (Photo by Jack Deutsch.)

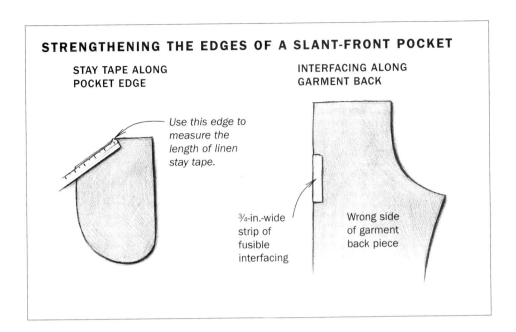

STRENGTHENING THE EDGES OF A SLANT-FRONT POCKET

STAY TAPE ALONG POCKET EDGE

Use this edge to measure the length of linen stay tape.

INTERFACING ALONG GARMENT BACK

¾-in.-wide strip of fusible interfacing

Wrong side of garment back piece

SEWING A SLANT-FRONT POCKET

To construct a slant-front pocket, proceed as follows.

1. Make all necessary waist and hip alterations on the garment and pocket pieces.

2. Place the pocket underlay right sides together on the garment front; pin. Cut a length of linen stay tape the length of the pocket opening—slant-front pocket openings are most often "off-grain" and will stretch out of shape, so don't cut the tape to match the fabric piece; instead, use the pattern to determine how much tape you need (see the left drawing above). Position the tape along the seam line of the underlay and garment front. It's okay if the tape is a bit short. Pin in place, matching end points and easing the stay tape in place along the seam line. If you are a novice pocket maker, baste the linen tape in place before you sew. Then stitch the seam through all three layers, using a ⅝-in. seam.

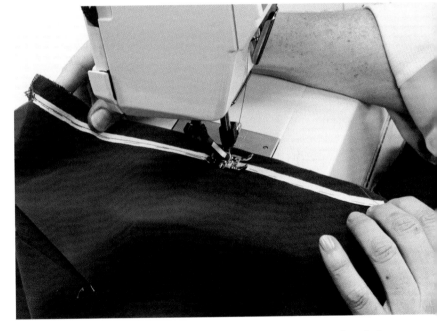

Position and sew stay tape along the seam line of the underlay and pocket front to keep the opening from stretching.

3. Press the pocket underlay away from the garment front, and press all seam allowances toward the pocket underlay (see the drawing below). Understitch the seam allowances: Sew both seam allowances onto the pocket underlay approximately ⅛ in. from the seam line. Trim, grading the seam allowances so that the seam allowance closest to the top of the garment is the longest. If you have never graded seam allowances before, this is a technique used to eliminate bulk: Flip the garment into its finished position. You will notice that both seam allowances are right next to each other. Check out which of these seam allowances is next to the top side of the garment. This seam allowance is trimmed a bit (about ¼ in.), but the second seam allowance is trimmed a lot—about ⅜ in.

4. Now press the underlay in place on the wrong side of the garment. Slant-front pockets are often topstitched. If you choose this design detail, top-stitch the edge of the pocket/garment front now.

5. If there are construction details such as darts in the pocket side front piece, construct them before attaching the pocket/garment front.

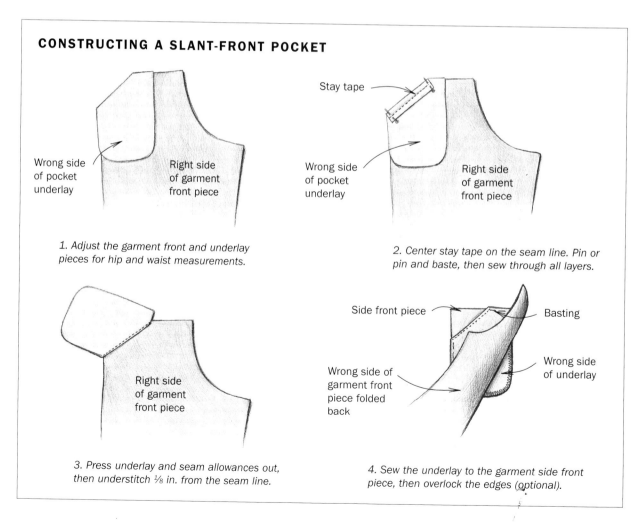

CONSTRUCTING A SLANT-FRONT POCKET

Wrong side of pocket underlay

Right side of garment front piece

1. Adjust the garment front and underlay pieces for hip and waist measurements.

Stay tape

Wrong side of pocket underlay

Right side of garment front piece

2. Center stay tape on the seam line. Pin or pin and baste, then sew through all layers.

Right side of garment front piece

3. Press underlay and seam allowances out, then understitch ⅛ in. from the seam line.

Side front piece

Basting

Wrong side of garment front piece folded back

Wrong side of underlay

4. Sew the underlay to the garment side front piece, then overlock the edges (optional).

6. Working from the right side of the garment, position the garment side front piece partly under the pocket/garment front, matching notches along the waistline edge and the side seam (see the photo below). Note that the pocket is not flat but generally has some curve to it. Pin or pin and baste the garment side front to the pocket garment/front.

7. At this point you will complete the pocket bag: Fold back the garment/pocket front and match the unsewn, curved edge of the underlay to the unattached edges of the garment side front. Sew together using a ⅝-in. seam allowance. If you wish, finish the seam using an overlock machine.

8. If you've decided to add a ¾-in. by 4-in. strip of fusible interfacing to the garment side back seam allowance, do it now, before attaching the completed garment front with pocket to the garment back at the side seam (see the right drawing on p. 45). Fuse the strip in place on the wrong side of the side seam on the garment back.

9. Pin, then baste the pocket back in position along the waistline edge. Pin or pin and baste the pocket back in position along the side seam. Anchor the side of the pocket in the garment side seam, and anchor the top of the pocket in the garment waistband.

Waistband Concealed in a Slant-Front Pocket

One of the most popular adaptations of a slant-front pocket is the waistband opening concealed in a slant-front pocket. Garments constructed with this detail do not require a zipper, so for many sewers, this means "easy."

As with the slant-front pocket discussed on p. 44, the pieces for this pocket type consist of the pocket/garment front, the underlay, and the garment side front/pocket back. It is very important to use stay tape—you don't want the pocket you are "stepping through" when you put on the garment to sag or stretch out of shape. The garment will be finished with a waistband that extends across the top of the garment side front/pocket back, around the garment waist, and across the top of the pocket front.

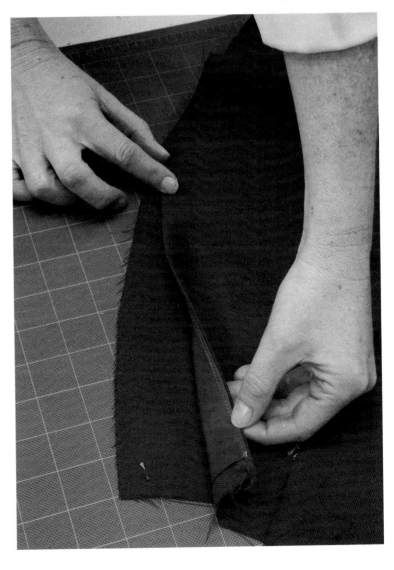

Position the garment side front piece under the pocket/garment front, matching notches and markings.

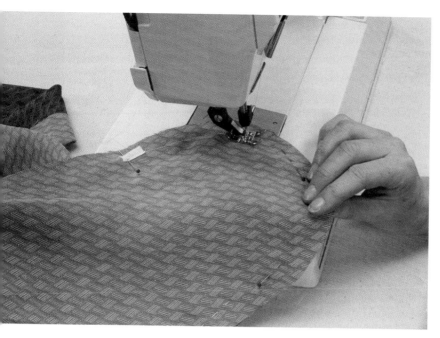

A piece of stay tape at the beginning of the stitching line will keep the pocket seam from tearing.

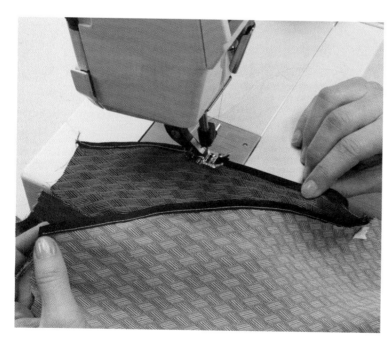

Binding the sewn edges of the pocket bag adds an elegant touch.

SEWING A SLANT-FRONT POCKET WITH WAISTLINE CLOSURE

Follow the steps here to construct this pocket.

1. Begin construction by transferring all waist and hip alterations to the pattern pieces. Cut and mark the pieces precisely.

2. Position the pocket underlay right sides together on the garment front, centering a piece of stay tape along the seam line. Pin together, and baste if necessary, then stitch through all three layers, using a ⅝-in. seam allowance.

3. Press the pocket underlay away from the garment front, and press all seam allowances toward the pocket underlay. Understitch the seam allowances to the underlay. Trim, grading the seam allowances so that the seam allowance closest to the top of the garment is the longest. Then press the seam allowances and underlay in place.

4. With right sides together, position the pocket/garment front on the garment side front, matching notches. Baste in place. Complete the right pocket as you would any slant-front pocket (see pp. 44-47). For the left pocket, which is the garment opening, align the bottom edges of the garment side front and the bottom edge of the underlay, adding a piece of stay tape or a small square of interfacing at the beginning of your stitching to prevent the seam from raveling or tearing (see the top photo at left). Complete sewing the pocket bag.

5. Clean-finish each of the unsewn seam allowances. I fold each seam allowance in half and half again, which is about ¼ in, and topstitch. Or you can bind the edges with rayon seam binding, which is approximately ½ in. wide and comes in more colors than you can imagine. (Be sure to use rayon seam binding, as polyester seam binding has a rigid edge and won't fold or press in half.) Prepare by folding and pressing the seam binding so that it's almost in half—one side should be wider than the other. Slip the seam binding over the edge of the seam, with the wider "half" of the seam binding on the side of the seam allowance that won't show. Sitch right along the edge of the seam binding on the top (see the bottom photo on the facing page); you will catch the wider half as you sew. This is one of my favorite finishes.

6. With right sides together, baste the side seam edges of the pocket/garment front and underlay to the pocket back.

7. Sew the left side seam of the garment. If you wish, interface the garment back seam allowance where it will meet the bottom edge of the pocket before sewing. I always include this step since the combination of lots of layers of fabric can make the side seam wavy or distorted; plus, it's not a difficult or time-consuming step to take.

8. Anchor the top of the pocket in the waistband by attaching the waistband all around the top of the garment from the pocket/garment front to the garment side front.

DESIGNER IN-SEAM POCKETS

There is no mystery to the pockets of designers, only imagination. What comes to my mind when I consider the in-seam pockets of designers I admire are the fantastic art-to-wear pieces that sport interesting fabrication for pockets, welts, and piping—mixed and matched,

even unmatched, fabrics. Some of these pieces feature unusual seaming; some have stitched detail on the pockets themselves and on the fabric around them. The possibilities are limitless.

But these pockets contain the same elements as the basics: the pocket pieces attach to seams or are cut on the seams (even both can be present in one design); the pocket is anchored in a seam line, be it vertical, horizontal, diagonal, or curved. Some pockets are piped, and some have added welts or flaps.

A designer in-seam pocket is as easy to make as a basic in-seam pocket. Here the pocket is placed in a curved seam line. (Photo by Jack Deutsch.)

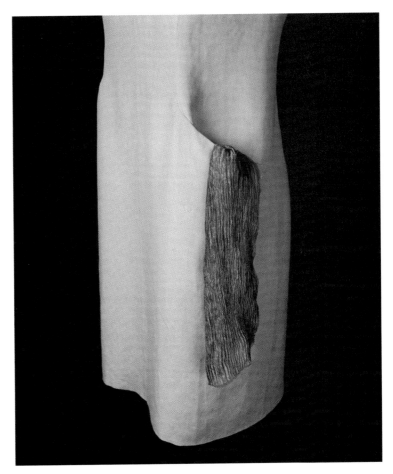

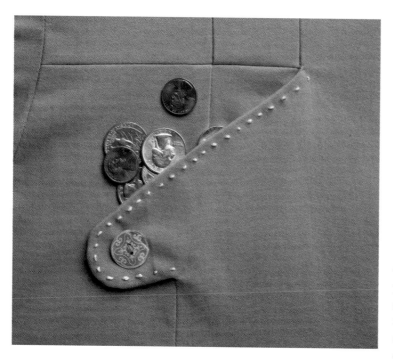

This designer in-seam pocket includes a shaped extension, detailed with contrasting-thread stitching. (Photo by Jack Deutsch.)

When you discover these pockets on ready-to-wear, study the lines of the garments and pull the pockets inside out. What fabric has been used where, and how was it attached? You can duplicate the look of designer garments by following the basic steps you have learned for side-seam pockets and slant-front pockets.

For the most part, the in-seam pockets we have been talking about so far have been in side seams. But there is an entire world of in-seam pockets that are in horizontal or diagonal seams. Where would American sportswear be without some variation of the car coat sporting a pocket apparently dropped in a seam line? By adding a welt, these pockets can look like the more difficult to construct welt pockets, but they are no more difficult to construct than the basic side-seam pockets.

Look for horizontal in-seam pockets in ready-to-wear and also in patterns. In ready-to-wear, this pocket can be spot-

ted by checking out the detail lines on the face of the garment. In a pattern, look at the line drawings—the pattern pieces will be different. In a jacket, for example, there will be the upper jacket which may (or may not) include the pocket back, the lower jacket, the pocket piece(s), and sometimes a welt.

SEWING A FRENCH-SEAMED SIDE POCKET

One of the most attractive in-seam pocket variations I have found is in couture garments from some of the Japanese designers. These garments are quite simple in shape but are distinguished by great finishing details: Seams are finished, edges are piped or bound, closures are hidden away or boldly part of the design. The pocket detail that has attracted my attention is the side-seam pocket that is French-seamed. These pockets have no raw edges when finished, and thus the garment is as beautiful on the inside as on the outside.

Construct this pocket as follows:
1. Cut out the pocket pieces and garment pieces. Then mark the pocket opening on both the pocket pieces and the garment pieces. These markings are essential.
2. With right sides together, position each pocket piece on each garment piece as you would if you were constructing the basic side-seam pocket. Sew each pocket piece in place using a ½-in. to ⅜-in. seam allowance, but sew only between the markings indicating the pocket opening. Do not attach the pocket pieces from end to end as you would with the basic side-seam pocket.
3. Clip straight in from the seam allowance to the ends of the pocket opening—exactly where you have started and stopped stitching.

CONSTRUCTING A FRENCH-SEAMED SIDE POCKET

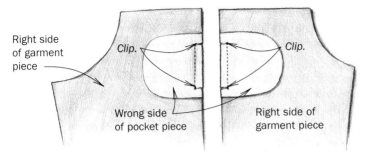

Right side
of garment
piece

Clip.

Clip.

Wrong side
of pocket piece

Right side of
garment piece

*1. Sew each pocket piece in place
on each garment piece only between
the pocket opening markings.*

Right side
of garment
piece

Right side
of garment
piece

*2. Finish the pocket attachment seams,
then press the pocket pieces out.*

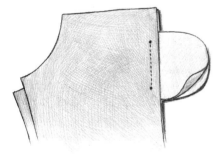

*3. Position the garment pieces with
wrong sides together.*

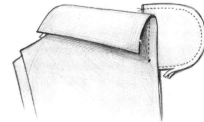

*4. Sew the pocket pieces together using
a ¼-in. seam allowance, then trim the
seam allowance.*

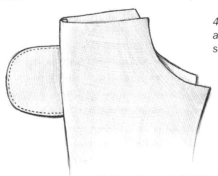

*5. Turn the pocket right side out, then sew around
the pocket bag using a ¼-in. seam allowance.*

4. Before continuing with the pocket, I usually finish the pocket attachment seams using the flat-fell seam technique described on pp. 38-39. Then press the pocket pieces out, toward the side of the garment.

5. Pin, then sew the pocket pieces wrong sides together all around the pocket bag using a 1/4-in. seam allowance. Press.

6. Trim the seam allowances a bit (see the drawing on p. 51). This is a good idea because your next stitching line will also be 1/4 in., and you want to fully encase the stitching you just completed.

7. Now turn the pocket right side out and press again. Align the garment side seams and the pocket edges. Pin or pin and baste. Then sew, again sewing only around the pocket bag using a 1/4-in. seam allowance.

8. Your pocket is now complete! Finish the garment side seams. If your pocket pieces have a waistband extension, anchor the top of the pocket in the garment waistband.

Almost any pocket can be finished this way. Remember that a French seam is constructed by first sewing *wrong* sides together, then by turning the garment so the right sides are together and the first seam is encased in the second seam. When the pocket is pushed into place, there are no raw edges, just a lovely, smooth pocket.

SEWING A HORIZONTAL IN-SEAM POCKET

The technique for constructing a horizontal in-seam pocket is a good one to have in your repertoire. This pocket is more difficult to construct than a basic side-seam pocket because the pocket is constructed as part of the garment. Careful marking is the key, and knowing how to work with a square corner is essential.

The pieces consist of the garment front, the garment side with cut-on pocket, and the pocket underlay. It is recommended that lining fabric or pocketing material be used for the underlay since this piece is positioned between two pieces of fashion fabric. You really don't want a "bulked-up" pocket, especially if it's right along your hip line!

Here are the construction steps.

1. After cutting the garment pieces, carefully mark all notches and dots. If you are like me, you will snip the notches and tailor-tack the dots. You may note that the dots are different sizes; if so, tailor-tack the large ones with one color thread and the smaller ones with a second color thread.

2. Look for the dot on the side of the garment front where the seam lines intersect. This is the pivot point for the square corner and needs your attention before any further sewing. Sew small reinforcing stitches for about 1/2 in. on each side of the dot, most easily accomplished by sewing to the dot, turning a square corner in the fabric, and continuing sewing 1/2 in. farther. You are only working with one layer of fabric here; this is a type of staystitching. Finish preparing the square corner by clipping to but not through the dot.

3. Next, position the underlay on the garment front piece with right sides

CONSTRUCTING A HORIZONTAL SIDE-SEAM POCKET

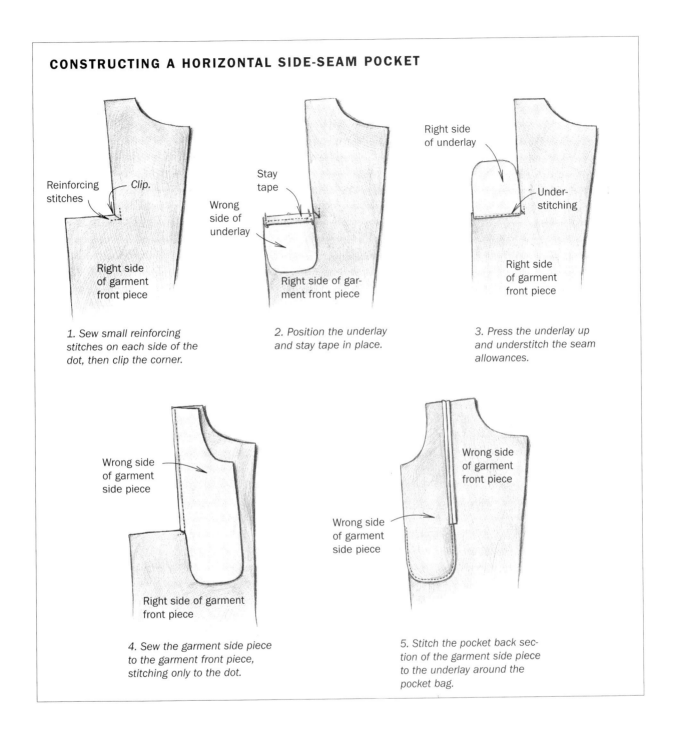

1. Sew small reinforcing stitches on each side of the dot, then clip the corner.

2. Position the underlay and stay tape in place.

3. Press the underlay up and understitch the seam allowances.

4. Sew the garment side piece to the garment front piece, stitching only to the dot.

5. Stitch the pocket back section of the garment side piece to the underlay around the pocket bag.

together. Position a piece of stay tape on top of the underlay. Pin or pin and baste the underlay and stay tape in place from dot to dot. Sew.

4. Press the underlay up, away from the stitching line. Press both seam allow-

ances toward the underlay. Understitch the seam allowances of the underlay by sewing both seam allowances to the underlay ⅛ in. away from the seam line.

5. Grade the seam allowances (see step 3 on p. 46).

6. Press the underlay into place on the wrong side of the garment front piece.

7. Sew the garment side piece to the garment front piece, right sides together, sewing only to the dot. Press the seam open and flip the pocket piece back into place.

8. Working from the wrong side of the garment, line up the edges of the pocket back and the underlay—this is the pocket bag. Stitch around the pocket bag to complete the pocket. If this is a jacket pocket, make a second row of stitches. (I hate jackets that have holes in the pockets!)

SEWING A HORIZONTAL IN-SEAM POCKET WITH WELT

The addition of a welt to a horizontal in-seam pocket can fool the world into thinking you have constructed a welt pocket!

1. Follow steps 1 and 2 on p. 52.

2. Construct the welt (see pp. 70-72).

3. Position the welt between the dots on the garment front piece. Baste in place. Position the underlay on top of the welt, and add stay tape as in step 3 on pp. 52-53.

4. Follow step 4 on p. 53. Note that I do not catch the welt in my understitching, nor do I grade the seam allowance of the welt.

5. Finish the horizontal in-seam pocket, following steps 5 through 8 on p. 53 and this page.

Piping

A couture look on slant-front pockets, as well as on in-seam pockets, is piping or cording the front of the pocket. To create this finish, first cut two strips of contrasting fabric on the bias, 1½ in. longer than the pocket opening and 2 in. wide. For example, for pockets that have 6-in. openings, cut two strips 7½ in. long and 2 in. wide. Cut a piece of cord for each pocket that is about 2 in. longer than the bias strip.

Position the cord in the center of the wrong side of the fabric strip, then fold the strip in half over the cord. Using a zipper foot, sew the strip next to, but not too close to, the cord. This seam creates the piping; the seam that attaches the piping to the garment will be the one that gets right up next to the cord.

Now sew your newly constructed piping in place between the underlay and the pocket/garment front. Position the piping so that the covered cord faces the hem of the garment (pin in place and flip back if you have trouble visualizing the finished position of the piping). You want the cord itself to be right up against the seam line, so fuss a bit here to get everything lined up just right. Skip using linen tape, as the piping will stabilize the edge. Pin or pin and baste, then sew the three elements together.

Finish constructing this slant-front pocket following steps 3 through 7 in the sidebar on p. 33. Before anchoring the pocket side in the side seam and the pocket top in the waistband, trim away all of the excess cord to eliminate bulk in the seam. Do this by pulling the cord out of the piping about ¾ in., trimming away ⅝ in., then carefully pushing the cord back into place.

CONSTRUCTING A HORIZONTAL IN-SEAM POCKET WITH WELT

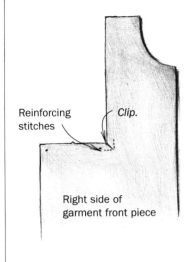

Reinforcing stitches

Clip.

Right side of garment front piece

1. Sew small reinforcing stitches on each side of the dot, then clip the corner.

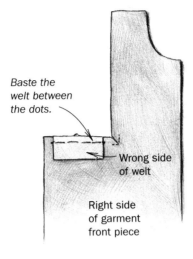

Baste the welt between the dots.

Wrong side of welt

Right side of garment front piece

2. Position and baste the welt in place.

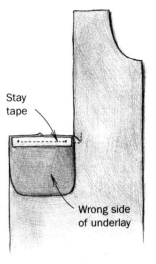

Stay tape

Wrong side of underlay

3. Position the underlay over the welt; add stay tape, then sew from dot to dot.

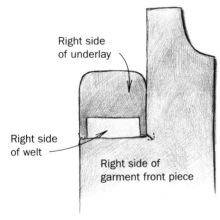

Right side of underlay

Right side of welt

Right side of garment front piece

4. Understitch the seam allowances of the underlay, being careful not to catch the welt in the understitching.

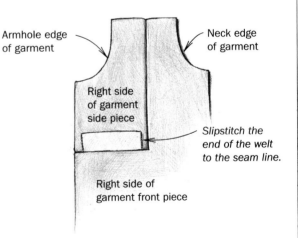

Armhole edge of garment

Neck edge of garment

Right side of garment side piece

Slipstitch the end of the welt to the seam line.

Right side of garment front piece

5. Sew the garment pieces together.

Jack Deutsch

INSET POCKETS

Regardless of how exacting your edgestitching abilities are to construct a perfect patch pocket, regardless of how carefully you mark, interface, and stitch to complete a perfect in-seam pocket, it is actually the inset pocket that defines the serious sewer. Sometimes called welt (because there is a rectangular welt at each pocket) or buttonhole (because the pockets resemble bound buttonholes) pockets, inset pockets require time and—let's face it—more attention to detail than either of the other pocket types mentioned. Plus, you have to cut a hole in your fabric, which is always scary and very permanent.

Inset pockets are little technical master-pieces. You need to give yourself permission to fuss, and then fuss as you go. In fact, before you start your first pocket, make yourself a few promises: promise to make a sample pocket before making the pockets in your garments; promise to baste and to use silk thread to baste every place you need to; promise to use a ruler or tape measure during the construction process; and finally, promise to rip out uneven stitches and resew as you go.

BASIC INSET POCKETS

Let me introduce you to the basic inset pocket—no lips, no welts, just a pocket on the wrong side of the garment accessible through an opening on the right side of the garment. When you see this pocket, a bit of the fabric behind the opening is visible from the front of the garment.

If this pocket type is not springing into your mind as you are reading this, don't be surprised. This pocket is like the unflavored version of a basic sauce. You don't find it in its unflavored state very often. I've seen this basic inset

pocket in ready-to-wear twice—once so inconspicuously in a plaid blouse that I had to look twice to notice it really was an inset pocket, and once in a blouse made of sheer fabric where it was the ultimate in elegance—the perfect pocket for that garment.

BEFORE YOU SEW

Constructing an inset pocket begins as most pocket construction does, with cutting the pieces and marking the fabric. To understand what pieces go where, put your hand in the pocket of the garment you are wearing. You will find that there is fabric that touches the back of your fingers and fabric that touches the front of your fingers. Each of these is a separate piece in a basic inset pocket: the pocket front piece and the pocket back piece.

These are the only pieces in the basic inset pocket. You have the option to cut the pocket front from fashion fabric if your fabric is lightweight, washable, or sheer. If you are making slacks or a jacket, you may cut the pocket front from lining or pocketing fabric. The pocket back should be cut from fashion fabric or a combination of fashion fabric and pocketing/lining—a faced piece.

How wide and how long are these pieces? The pocket pieces need to be wider than the pocket opening is long— 1½ in. provides fabric to seam and enough extra on each side to fuss with, even if some might be trimmed away in the finished pocket. The length of the pocket pieces needs to be equal to the pocket depth plus 2 in. to 3 in., with the pocket front piece a bit shorter than the pocket back. Therefore, for a 6-in.-wide pocket with a 5-in. depth, I would cut a pocket front piece 7½ in. wide and 7 in. long and a pocket back piece 7½ in. wide and 8 in. long.

POCKET BACK WITH FASHION FABRIC

Seam line

3 in. of fashion fabric

Turn under ¼ in. and topstitch.

Right side of pocketing/lining

The faced pocket back (a combination of fashion fabric and pocketing/lining) is constructed by basting a 3-in. piece of fashion fabric to a piece of pocketing/lining, wrong side to right side, along one end (see the drawing on the facing page). The opposite end of the fashion fabric is folded under ¼ in. and topstitched in place. For ladies' garments, unless the fabric is bulky, better ready-to-wear garments have pocket back pieces cut entirely from fashion fabric.

Since pockets, like hands, come in pairs (a standard in human anatomy, but hardly standard in garment design!), it is best to cut and sew pairs of pockets at the same time. You are more likely to have even pockets this way.

Marking the garment pieces is next. Make tailor tacks using silk thread at the ends of the opening for each pocket. (Eventually you will remove the tailor tacks, and silk thread will pull out more easily than thread with a stronger twist.) These will mark the ends of the line that is generally the top of the pocket. You will cut along this line, too. Once you have marked the garment pieces, construct darts or seams that are in the pocket area—the exception to the "pockets go first" rule. It is not unusual for inset pockets to span parts of darts and/or seams.

Next, interface the pocket opening on the garment. Position a small oval of fusible interfacing over the area that is the top of the pocket, including the tailor tacks, on the wrong side of the fabric (see the top photo at right).

Working from the wrong side of the garment, mark a line on the fusible interfacing between the tailor tacks, using a pencil or other non-penetrating marker. Then draw the end lines of the pocket. Again using silk thread, baste

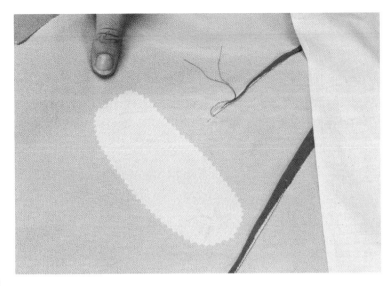

Fuse the interfacing right over the tailor tacks on the wrong side of the fabric.

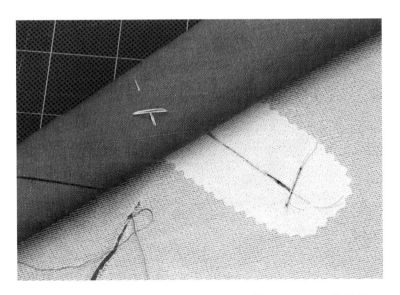

Baste along the pencil markings so that the markings appear on both the right and wrong side.

along the line marking and the end markings. Make your stitches even so that you can see the markings on both the right and the wrong sides of the fabric (see the bottom photo above).

SEWING A BASIC INSET POCKET

1. After the pocket pieces are cut out, you have to mark them before you can start constructing the pocket. On each pocket piece sew a row of machine stitches ¼ in. from one end; if the pocket back piece is a combination of fashion fabric and pocketing, you have basted the fabric to the lining on this end. Measure carefully and trim off ⅛ in. so that exactly ⅛ in. remains above the stitching line on each piece. The machine stitches are the guidelines for attaching the pocket pieces to the garment; the machine stitching marks the top of each of these pieces. (Note to experienced sewers: If I have just lost you after the trimming instructions, remember that this is the lipless "unflavored" inset pocket.)

2. Place the pocket pieces right sides together on the right side of the garment along the basted line marking the pocket opening. The pocket back is positioned with the top of the piece—remember the machine stitching marks the top—toward the pocket-placement line. The pocket front is positioned with the top of the piece toward the pocket-placement line. The raw edges of the pocket pieces abut the silk thread basting line on the garment.

3. Using silk thread, baste the pieces in place. Mark the end points on each side. There should be exactly ¼ in. between the two rows of machine stitching on the pocket pieces. Use a small ruler or tape measure to check that the two rows of machine stitches are an even ¼ in. apart from end point to end point. Pull out the stitches and rebaste the pieces if they are not an even distance apart (see the drawing below).

4. Once you are satisfied that your lines are even, machine-stitch each pocket piece in place along the stitching lines, stopping exactly at each end point.

5. Again examine your work. With a ruler or tape measure, check that the lines of stitching are perfectly parallel. Check also that the stitching starts and stops at each end point. Fuss if you need to, pulling out or adding a stitch or two

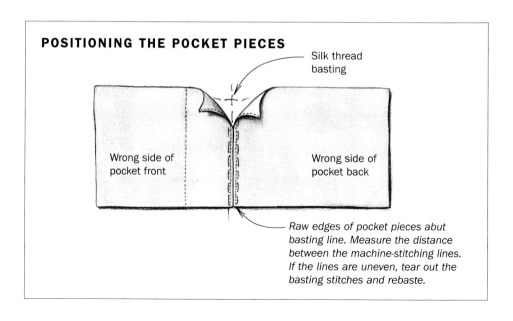

POSITIONING THE POCKET PIECES

Silk thread basting

Wrong side of pocket front

Wrong side of pocket back

Raw edges of pocket pieces abut basting line. Measure the distance between the machine-stitching lines. If the lines are uneven, tear out the basting stitches and rebaste.

CUTTING THE POCKET OPENING

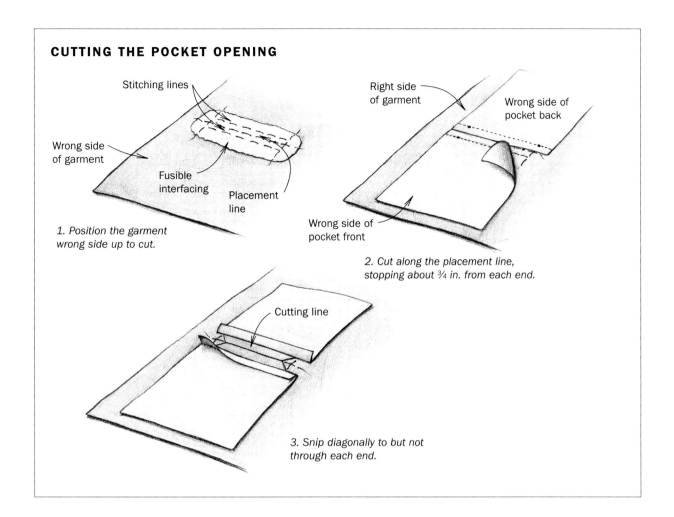

Stitching lines

Wrong side
of garment

Fusible
interfacing

Placement
line

*1. Position the garment
wrong side up to cut.*

Right side
of garment

Wrong side of
pocket back

Wrong side of
pocket front

*2. Cut along the placement line,
stopping about ¾ in. from each end.*

Cutting line

*3. Snip diagonally to but not
through each end.*

to make sure you are exactly at the ends of the line or resewing uneven parts. What makes these pockets look good is being as fussy as you can be right now—before you cut the garment—when you are easily able to correct unevenness and irregularities. If the stitching looks good, if the lines are straight, and if the stitches start and stop exactly at the end points, then it is time to cut.

6. Position the garment wrong side up, and starting in the middle of the basted line, use small, sharp scissors to cut along the line. Use your fingers to keep the seam allowances of the pocket pieces, which are on the right side of the

garment, out of the way. The basted line is going to be your cutting guide; it should be right in the middle of the space. Stop about ¾ in. from each end.

7. Now snip diagonally to but not through (these are what I call the magic words) each corner, so that there is a tiny triangle at each end, from the cutting line toward each corner (see the drawing above).

8. Push each pocket piece through the slash to the wrong side of the garment. Press the pocket flat, pressing both the pocket front piece and the pocket back piece toward the hem and pressing the

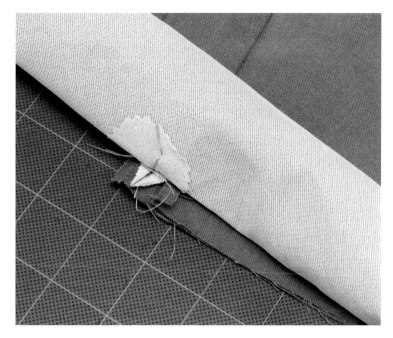

Fold the garment back to show the little triangle and the pocket seam allowance.

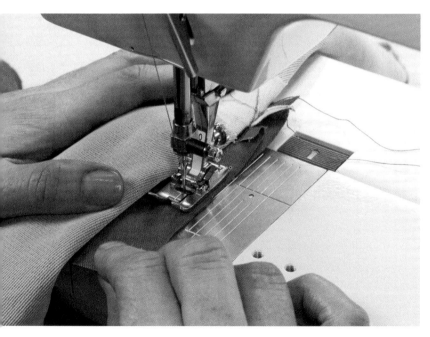

Stitch across the base of the triangle and around the pocket.

little triangles away from the pocket on each side. Make sure that no part of the triangles shows from the right side.

9. To secure the pocket back and pocket front pieces to finish the pocket bag, place the garment piece flat on your work surface, with the right side facing up. Fold the garment back, in line with the end of the pocket. You should see the little triangle on top of the evenly pressed seam allowances (see the top photo at left). Reach under on each side and give the pocket pieces a tug to pull them into place. Machine-baste along the base of the triangles, through all thicknesses, and along the side of the pocket pieces. Repeat this for the other end of the pocket.

10. Check the garment from the right side again. Does everything lie flat and look even? If so, fold the garment back again and stitch with smaller than normal stitches along the basted line at the base of one triangle, around the entire pocket, and across the base of the triangle on the other side of the pocket (see the bottom photo at left).

Some sewers like to anchor the triangles with multiple rows of small stitches. This is okay, but don't do this initially to anchor the triangles because all that back-and-forth stitching can pull them—and the pocket—out of position. Do it later when everything is already straight.

11. To finish the edges of this inset pocket, make a second row of machine stitches around the pocket bag and trim away any uneven edges and excess fabric. An optional finish is to zigzag or overlock the edges of the pocket bag.

Variations of the Basic Inset Pocket

Now that you know the construction techniques for a basic "unflavored" inset pocket, you are ready to construct the four most popular "flavored" versions—the single-lip pocket, the double-lip or buttonhole pocket, the welt pocket, and the buttonhole pocket with a flap. You will, for the most part, follow the steps for a basic inset pocket and add welt, lips, or flaps.

BEFORE YOU SEW

The preparation of the garment for any of these variations remains the same as the preparation of the garment for the basic inset pocket: Tailor-tack the ends of the pocket opening, construct darts or seams in the pocket area, and fuse an oval of interfacing on the wrong side of the garment in the pocket area. You will then draw the pocket-placement line and the pocket end lines, and trace the markings with silk thread, just as you did in the basic inset pocket instructions.

PREPARING THE PIECES

Cut the pocket back and pocket front pieces using the guidelines that the pieces need to be 1½ in. wider than the pocket opening is long and equal to the pocket depth plus 2 in. to 3 in.

MAKING LIPS OR WELTS

In inset pockets with lips or welts, the lips are rectangles that are folded, which singly or in pairs fill the inset opening exactly. ("Advanced" inset pockets can have all sort of things going on in the space we are calling the inset opening, including lips that don't fill the space. We'll get to that later.)

1. For a single-lip pocket, cut the lip piece as long as the pocket opening plus 1½ in. The width of a single lip piece is two times the size of the inset opening plus two ¼-in. seam allowances, plus a bit to allow for folding the piece. For example, the lip piece in a 6-in. pocket with a ½-in. finished lip is cut 1¾ in. wide and 7½ in. long.

For a double-lip pocket, cut two lip pocket pieces, each as long as the pocket opening plus 1½ in. The width of each lip piece is one-half the inset opening, times two, plus two ¼-in. seam allowances, plus a bit to allow for folding the piece. For example, the lip pieces in a 6-in. buttonhole pocket with ⅜-in. finished lips are each cut 1½ in. wide and 7½ in. long.

2. Press the pieces. For all lip pieces, follow this basic rule: Press, press, press, press, and press. You want to press all of the stretch out of these pieces now so they don't stretch when the pocket is finished.

3. Interfacing is optional. Some lips are completely interfaced, some half interfaced, and some not interfaced at all. If you choose to interface, do it before you fold and press the lips. Use lightweight fusible interfacing on the wrong side of the lip pieces.

4. Fold each lip piece in half after interfacing; press. Pound flat with a clapper.

MARKING THE PIECES

1. Mark the pocket back piece and the pocket front piece with a stay-stitching line that is ¼ in. from one edge. The stay-stitched edge is the top of the pocket piece. Measure with a small ruler to make sure your stitching is even, then trim excess fabric away. Tear out and restitch if the line is wavy or crooked.

2. Measuring from the folded edge of the lip piece, mark and sew a stay-stitching line that is the width of the

The Inset Pocket Opening

Whether you are constructing the unflavored, basic inset pocket or a buttonhole pocket with a flap, it is important to understand what the inset opening consists of.

Basically the inset opening is the distance between the two lines of machine stitching that are parallel to the basted pocket-placement line. The two lines of machine stitching are the attachment lines for the pocket back, lips, welts, and pocket front.

For a basic inset pocket, the inset opening is the amount of the pocket back piece that will be visible from the front of the garment, with no lips, flaps, or welts to hide the pocket back.

For a pocket with lips, the inset opening is exactly filled in by the width of the lip pieces. A single lip is the exact width of the opening; each lip in a double-lip buttonhole pocket fills exactly half the space.

For a welt pocket, the inset opening is not visible at all but is covered by the welt, which is usually larger than the distance between the stitching lines that attach the welt and the pocket back.

If you are asking what you do with this information now that you have added it to your bag of tricks, the answer is use it: Use it to calculate how far apart the stitching lines need to be for whatever finished lip width you want. For example, if you want the finished lips on your buttonhole pocket to be ¾ in. wide, the distance between the stitching lines of the lips has to be 1½ in.—each lip attached ¾ in. from the pocket-placement line. If you want a *single*, finished lip of ½ in., the distance between the stitching line on the single lip and the pocket back piece has to be ½ in., each element

attached ¼ in. from the pocket-placement line. If you are aiming for tiny lips, make the stitching lines ¼ in. apart and attach two lips ⅛ in. from the placement line.

To construct a pocket with a welt, the seam allowances of the welt and the pocket back piece can be ¼ in. apart because the welt is wider than the opening and because none of the pocket back will be visible in the finished pocket.

There is potential here for some great design: One example is to make lips that are ½ in. or ¾ in. wide and position them at each end of a large, visible pocket back. The stitching lines are usually parallel and as far apart as you want the pocket back to show. Make the pocket back in a contrasting fabric—maybe the fabric you used for the skirt that goes with the jacket. Or use bias grain for the pocket back.

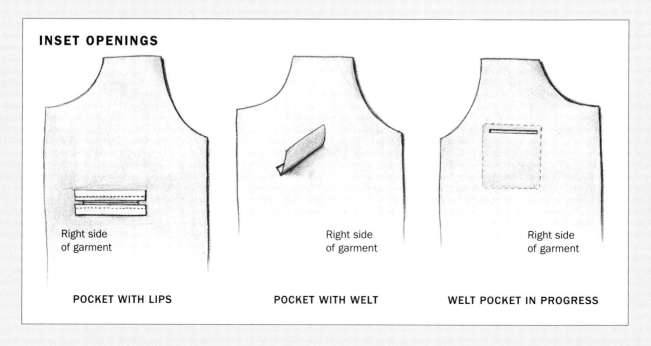

INSET OPENINGS

Right side of garment

Right side of garment

Right side of garment

POCKET WITH LIPS

POCKET WITH WELT

WELT POCKET IN PROGRESS

finished lip. For our example of a ½-in. finished lip, the stay-stitching line will be ½ in. away from the fold. Measure with a small ruler to make sure your stitching is even; tear out and restitch if the line is wavy or crooked. Trim the raw edges of the lip piece to an even ¼ in.

3. Cut and mark each pocket piece following the directions on p. 63. Mark welts and flaps by sewing a stay-stitching line ¼ in. from the raw edge. Measure with a small ruler to make sure your stitching is even; tear out and restitch if the line is wavy or crooked.

COMPLETING THE POCKET

Now follow one of the variations here—single lip inset, buttonhole, welt, or buttonhole with flap—to complete your pocket.

Single-lip pocket

1. Mark the pocket-placement line on the garment with tailor tacks.
2. Interface the wrong side of the garment with an oval of fusible interfacing large enough to cover the pocket-placement line and the end lines of the pocket.
3. Mark the pocket-placement line and end lines on the fusible interfacing, then trace with a silk thread basting line. Make sure the stitches are even and show on the right side of the garment.
4. Cut and interface the lip. Fold it in half and press. Mark with a line of stay stitching.
5. Cut the pocket back piece from fashion fabric or a combination of fashion fabric and lining fabric. Mark the piece with stay stitching along one edge.
6. Cut the pocket front piece from fashion fabric or lining fabric. Mark the piece with stay stitching along one edge.
7. Check all stay-stitching lines. Pull out wavy or crooked stitches and resew if necessary. Trim seam allowances to ¼ in.
8. Working on the right side of the garment with right sides together, position the pocket back piece parallel to the basted placement line. The stay-stitched edge, which is the top of the

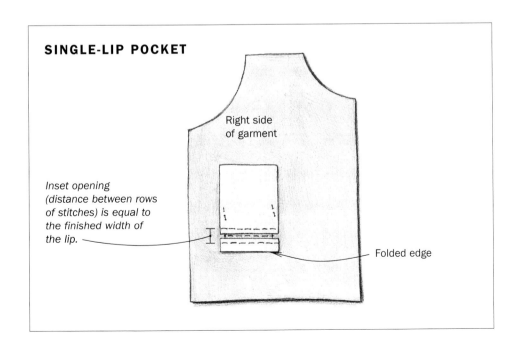

SINGLE-LIP POCKET

Right side of garment

Inset opening (distance between rows of stitches) is equal to the finished width of the lip.

Folded edge

Making Lips from Bias

Lips are constructed with fashion fabric and can be cut on the lengthwise grain, on the crosswise grain, or on the bias. Cutting on the bias can save you from having to match the stripe or plaid. Variations in grain lines are decorative and add interest to a garment and can be reason enough to cut the lips on the bias. From the very beginning, though, you have to take the stretchiness of bias into consideration. For bias-cut lips, pressing reshapes the piece, so after pressing, recut the lips to the size you need. Follow these steps.

1. Cut bias lips from a piece of fabric wider and longer than the finished pieces need to be.

2. Because bias stretches, press and stretch the bias pieces as much as you can, in every direction. You will note that the strips will get longer and narrower as you stretch them. After the pieces have cooled and dried, recut the lips to the size you need.

3. Interfacing is not optional! Fuse lightweight interfacing to the wrong side of the lip pieces.

4. Fold the lip pieces in half and pound with a clapper.

pocket back piece, should be close to the basted placement line. Pin and baste in place with silk thread. Mark the ends of the pocket with pins or additional basting.

9. Position the lip on the right side of the garment parallel to the basted pocket-placement line. The folded edge of the lip should be toward the hem of the garment and the stay-stitching line should be close to the basted placement line (see the drawing on p. 65). Pin and baste in place with silk thread. Mark the ends of the pocket with pins or additional basting.

10. Check the distance between the basting lines attaching the pocket back pieces and the lip: This distance should equal the finished width of the lip. The lines should be straight, and the end marks should be directly opposite each other.

11. Stitch the pocket back piece in place along the basting line, stopping and starting at each end mark. Stitch the lip in place along the basting line, stopping and starting at each end mark.

Check your stitching to make sure it is straight and even. Check to make sure that the end of each stitching line is directly opposite the other. Take out uneven stitches and resew if necessary.

12. Working from the wrong side of the garment, use small, sharp scissors to cut along the pocket-placement line between the two stitching lines, taking care not to cut the seam allowances of the lips. Stop ¾ in. from each end. Cut diagonally to but not through the end of each stitching line to make triangles at each end of the pocket-placement line.

13. From the right side of the garment, push the pocket back piece to the wrong side of the garment. From the right side of the garment, push the lip into position. Tuck the edges of the pieces to the wrong side of the garment. With silk thread, whipstitch the top of the lip to the top of the inset opening. Press the pocket flat.

14. On the wrong side of the garment, pull a bit on the edges of the lip and make sure the triangles are pressed to each side of the pocket.

15. Working on the wrong side of the garment, attach the pocket front piece by positioning the stay stitching on the top of the pocket front along the seam allowance of the lip. Pin and check that the lip seam allowance is between the pocket front piece and the garment and not inside the pocket. Sew along the stay-stitching line. Press.

16. Lay the garment flat, right side up. Fold back the garment in line with the end of the pocket so you see the small triangle neatly on top of the end of the lip and the seam allowances of the pocket pieces. Baste along the base of each triangle to anchor the pocket in position.

17. Check one last time that the lip is straight and the pocket is flat. Sew across the base of the triangle on one edge of the pocket. Sew along the edges of the pocket pieces around to the other triangle. Sew along the base of the triangle on the second side.

18. Make a second row of stitches next to the first one around the pocket bag. Trim the edges so they are even. Sew additional rows of stitches across the triangles if you wish.

Buttonhole pocket

1. Mark the pocket-placement line on the garment with tailor tacks.

2. Interface the wrong side of the garment with an oval of fusible interfacing large enough to cover the pocket-placement line and the end lines of the pocket.

3. Mark the pocket-placement line and end lines on the fusible interfacing, then trace with a silk thread basting line. Make sure the stitches are even and show on the right side of the garment.

4. Cut and interface the lips. Fold them in half and press. Mark each with a stay-stitching line.

5. Cut the pocket back piece from fashion fabric or a combination of fashion

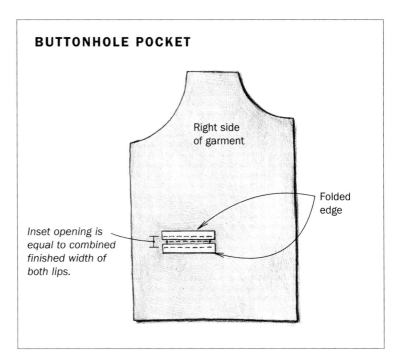

BUTTONHOLE POCKET

Right side of garment

Folded edge

Inset opening is equal to combined finished width of both lips.

fabric and lining fabric. Mark the piece with stay stitching along one edge.

6. Cut the pocket front piece from fashion fabric or lining fabric. Mark the piece with stay stitching along one edge.

7. Check all stay-stitching lines. Pull out wavy or crooked stitches and resew if necessary. Trim seam allowances to ¼ in.

8. Position both lips on the right side of the garment, parallel to the basted pocket-placement line. The folded edges of the lips should face away from the placement line (see the drawing above). Pin and baste in place with silk thread. Mark the ends of the pocket with pins or additional basting.

9. Check the distance between the basting lines attaching the lips: This distance should be equal to the combined finished widths of the lips. The lines should be straight, and the end lines should be directly opposite each other.

10. Stitch the lips in place along the basting, stopping and starting at each end line. Check your stitching to make sure it is straight and even. Check to make sure that the end lines are directly opposite each other. Take out uneven stitches and resew if necessary.

11. Working from the wrong side of the garment, use small, sharp scissors to cut along the pocket-placement line between the two stitching lines, taking care not to cut the seam allowances of the lips. Stop ¾ in. from each end. Cut diagonally to but not through the end of each stitching line to make triangles at each end of the pocket-placement line.

12. Push the lips into position, tucking the edges of the pieces to the wrong side of the garment. With silk thread, whipstitch the lips together where they meet. Press the pocket flat.

13. On the wrong side of the garment, pull a bit on the edges of the lips and make sure the triangles are pressed to each side of the pocket.

14. Working on the wrong side of the garment, attach the pocket front piece by positioning the stay stitching on the top of the piece along the seam allowance of the lower lip. Pin and check that the lip is between the pocket front piece and the garment and not inside the pocket. Sew along the stay-stitching line (see the drawing below). Press.

15. Also on the wrong side of the garment, attach the pocket back piece by positioning the stay stitching on the top of the piece along the seam allowance of the upper lip. Pin and check that the lip is between the pocket

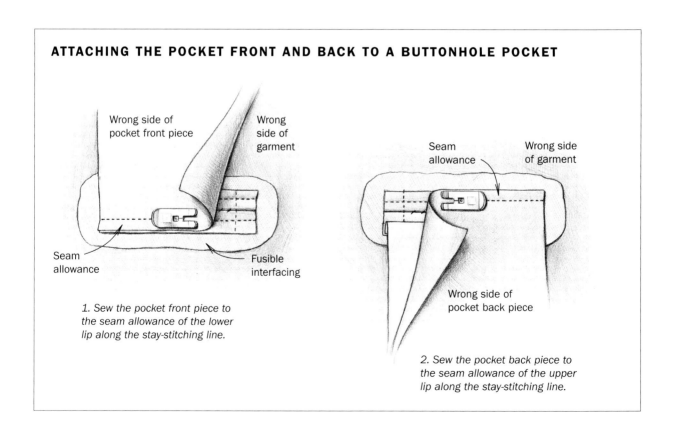

ATTACHING THE POCKET FRONT AND BACK TO A BUTTONHOLE POCKET

Wrong side of pocket front piece

Wrong side of garment

Seam allowance

Fusible interfacing

1. Sew the pocket front piece to the seam allowance of the lower lip along the stay-stitching line.

Seam allowance

Wrong side of garment

Wrong side of pocket back piece

2. Sew the pocket back piece to the seam allowance of the upper lip along the stay-stitching line.

back piece and the garment and not inside the pocket. Sew along the stay-stitching line. Press.

16. Lay the garment flat, right side up. Fold back the garment in line with the end of the pocket—you should see the small triangle neatly on top of the ends of the lip and the seam allowances of the pocket pieces. Baste along the base of each triangle to anchor the pocket in position.

17. Check one last time that the lips are straight and the pocket is flat. Sew across the base of the triangle on one end of the pocket, then stitch the edges of the pocket pieces together, sewing around the pocket bag to the other triangle. Sew along the base of the triangle on the second side.

18. Make a second row of stitches next to the first one around the pocket bag. Trim the edges so they are even. Sew additional rows of stitches across the triangles if you wish.

Welt pocket

1. Mark the pocket-placement line on the garment with tailor tacks.

2. Interface the wrong side of the garment with an oval of fusible interfacing large enough to cover the pocket-placement line and the end lines of the pocket.

3. Mark the pocket-placement line and end lines on the fusible interfacing, then trace with a silk thread basting line. Make sure the stitches are parallel (see the photo above) and show on the right side of the garment.

4. Cut out and construct the welt so that the finished welt will fit the width of the pocket opening exactly. Follow the directions on p. 88.

5. Cut the pocket back piece from fashion fabric or a combination of fashion

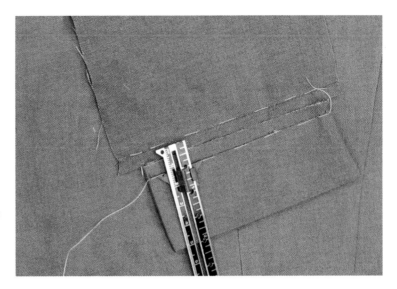

Use a seam guide (shown), a see-through ruler, or other small measuring device to check that the basting lines are perfectly parallel.

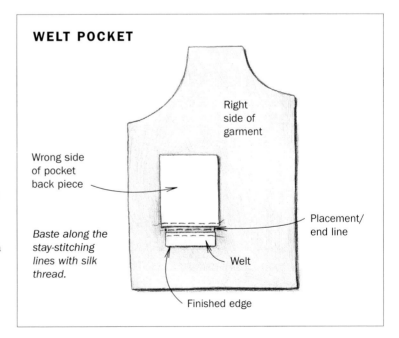

WELT POCKET

Right side of garment

Wrong side of pocket back piece

Placement/ end line

Baste along the stay-stitching lines with silk thread.

Welt

Finished edge

fabric and lining fabric. Mark the piece with stay stitching along one edge.

6. Cut the pocket front piece from fashion fabric or lining fabric. Mark the piece with stay stitching along one edge.

7. Check to make sure all stay-stitching lines are ¼ in. from the edges. Pull out wavy or crooked stitches and resew if necessary. Trim seam allowances to ¼ in.

8. Working on the right side of the garment with right sides together, position the pocket back piece ¼ in. away from the basted placement line. The stay-stitched edge, which is the top of the pocket back piece, should be close to the basted placement line. Pin and baste in place with silk thread. Mark the ends of the pocket with pins or additional basting.

9. Position the welt upside down on the right side of the garment between the end lines (see the drawing on p. 69). (By upside down I mean so that the finished edge of the welt is toward the hem of the garment if it will be toward the top of the garment when finished.) The stay stitching should be ¼ in. away from the basted pocket-placement line. Pin and baste in place with silk thread.

10. Check the distance between the basting lines attaching the pocket back piece and the lip: This distance should be exactly ½ in. The lines should be straight, and the end lines of the pocket back piece should be directly opposite the edges of the welt.

11. Stitch the pocket back piece in place along the basting line, stopping and starting at each end line (see the left photo below). Stitch the welt in place along the basting line, stopping and starting at each edge. Check your stitching to make sure it is straight and even. Check to make sure that the end lines are directly opposite each other. Take out uneven stitches and resew where necessary.

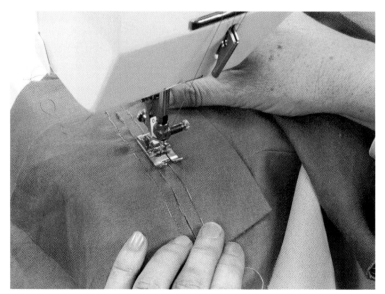

Stitch the pocket back piece to the garment then stitch the welt to the garment through all layers, from end mark to end mark along the basting line.

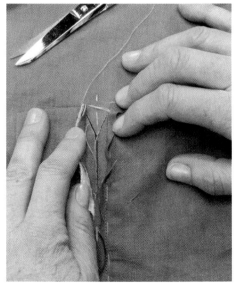

Cut along the pocket-placement line, keeping the welt and the pocket back piece out of the way.

12. Working from the wrong side of the garment, use small, sharp scissors to cut along the pocket-placement line between the two stitching lines, taking care not to cut the seam allowances of the pieces. Stop ¾ in. from each end. Cut diagonally to but not through the end of each stitching line to make triangles at each end of the pocket-placement line (see the right photo on the facing page).

13. Push the pocket back piece to the wrong side of the garment (see the photo below). On the right side of the garment, flip the welt into position. Tuck the edges of the pocket back piece to the wrong side of the garment. With silk thread, loosely whipstitch the top of the welt to the garment. Press the pocket flat.

14. On the wrong side of the garment, pull on the edges of the pocket back piece and make sure the triangles are pressed to each side of the pocket.

15. Also on the wrong side of the garment, attach the pocket front piece by positioning the stay stitching on the top of the piece along the seam allowance of the welt. Pin and check that the welt is between the pocket front piece and the garment and not inside the pocket (see the photo on p. 72). Sew along the stay-stitching line. Press.

16. Lay the garment flat, right side up. Fold back the garment in line with the end of the pocket—you should see the small triangle neatly on top of the seam allowances of the pocket pieces. Baste along the base of each triangle to anchor the pocket in position.

17. Check one last time that the pocket is flat. Sew across the base of the triangle on one edge of the pocket. Sew along the edges of the pocket pieces around to the other triangle. Sew along the base of the triangle on the second side.

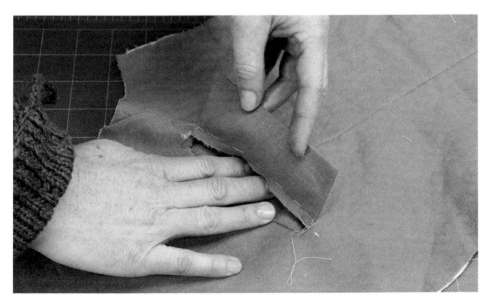

Gently push the pocket back piece through the opening.

18. Make a second row of stitches next to the first one around the pocket bag. Trim the edges so they are even (see the drawing below). Sew additional rows of stitches across the triangles if you wish.
19. Slipstitch the sides of the welt to hide the inset opening (see the top photo on the facing page) or use small

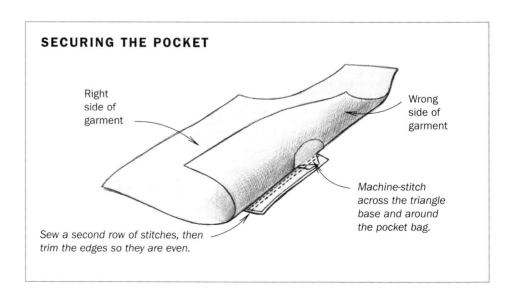

Match the stay-stitching line on the right side of the pocket front piece to the seam allowance of the welt, making sure that the welt's seam allowance is between the pocket front piece and the wrong side of the garment.

diagonal stitches on the wrong side of the garment, taking care not to pull the stitches too tight.

Double-lip buttonhole pocket with a flap
1. Mark the pocket-placement line on the garment with tailor tacks.
2. Interface the wrong side of the garment with an oval of fusible interfacing large enough to cover the pocket-placement line and the end lines of the pockets.
3. Mark the pocket-placement line and end lines on the fusible interfacing, then trace with a silk thread basting line. Make sure the stitches are even and show on the right side of the garment.
4. Cut and interface the lips. Fold them in half and press. Mark each with a stay-stitching line.
5. Cut the pocket back piece from fashion fabric or a combination of fashion fabric and lining fabric. Mark the piece with stay stitching along one edge.
6. Cut the pocket front piece from fashion fabric or lining fabric. Mark the piece with stay stitching along one edge.

SECURING THE POCKET

Right side of garment

Wrong side of garment

Machine-stitch across the triangle base and around the pocket bag.

Sew a second row of stitches, then trim the edges so they are even.

---

7. Cut and construct the flap so that the finished flap will fit the pocket exactly—the flap must fit between the end lines. Follow the directions for construction method 1 on p. 88.

8. Check all stay-stitching lines. Pull out wavy or crooked stitches and resew if necessary. Trim seam allowances to ¼ in.

9. Position both lips on the right side of the garment, parallel to the basted pocket-placement line. The folded edges of the lips should face away from the placement line. Pin and baste in place with silk thread. Mark the ends of the pocket with pins or additional basting.

10. Check the distance between the basting lines attaching the lips: This distance should be equal to the combined finished widths of the lips. The lines should be straight, and the end lines should be directly opposite each other.

11. Stitch the lips in place along the basting, stopping and starting at each end mark. Check your stitching to make sure it is straight and even. Check to make sure that the ends are directly opposite each other. Take out uneven stitches and resew where necessary.

12. Working from the wrong side of the garment, use small, sharp scissors to cut along the pocket-placement line between the two stitching lines, taking care not to cut the seam allowances of the lips. Stop ¾ in. from each end. Cut diagonally to but not through the end of each stitching line to make triangles at each end of the pocket-placement line.

13. Push the lips into position, tucking the edges of the pieces to the wrong side of the garment.

14. On the wrong side of the garment, pull a bit on the edges of the lips and make sure the triangles are pressed to each side of the pocket.

15. On the right side of the garment, slip the flap into place between the lips (see the photo on p. 74). Pin. Turn the garment over and repin the raw edge of

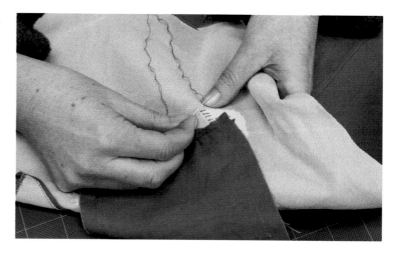

Anchor the welt in place by hand with silk thread.

One variation of an inset pocket is a buttonhole pocket with a flap. The pocket bag here is a single faced piece that combines pocketing material with fashion fabric.

ATTACHING THE FLAP

Baste the flap to the seam allowance of the upper lip.

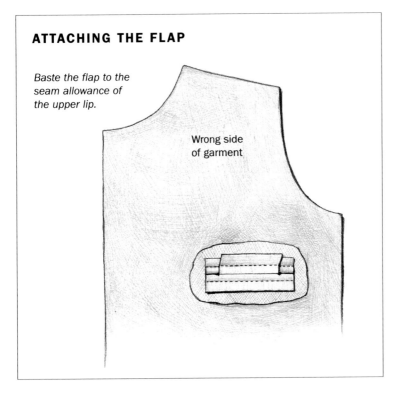

Wrong side of garment

the flap to the seam allowance of the upper lip. Stitch in place (see the drawing at left).

16. Working on the wrong side of the garment, attach the pocket front piece by positioning the stay stitching on the top of the piece along the seam allowance of the lower lip. Pin and check that the lip is between the pocket front piece and the garment and not inside the pocket. Sew along the stay-stitching line. Press.

17. Position the stay stitching on the right side of the pocket back piece along the seam allowance of the upper lip, where the flap is also attached. Pin and check that the lip is between the pocket back piece and the garment and not inside the pocket. Sew along the stay-stitching line. Press.

18. Lay the garment flat, right side up. Fold back the garment in line with the end of the pocket—you should see the small triangle neatly on top of the ends of the lips and the seam allowances of the pocket pieces. Baste along the base of each triangle to anchor the pocket in position.

Pockets on a Slant

Very often a pair of slacks, a jacket, or a coat has an inset pocket on a diagonal placement line or the pocket is horizontal but the end lines are diagonal. In both cases, you need to pay attention to the finished position of the welt or lips before cutting along the pocket-placement line and before cutting the little triangles so that the slash doesn't show.

When the pocket is slanted, the pieces are parallel to the pocket-placement line, but not lined up directly across from each other. The key is knowing where the end marks are.

After you have stitched the welt and pocket back, the lip and pocket back, or both lips of a buttonhole pocket in place, flip the garment to the wrong side. Three lines should be visible: two stitching lines and the basted pocket-placement line. You have to find where the pocket-placement line is common to both pieces before you cut along that line—and you have to stop ¾ in. from each end so you can cut the triangles.

I like to take a pencil and draw the end lines on the interfacing by connecting the ends of the stitching lines. I can then draw the triangles before the placement line and the triangles are cut. This way, I am sure that there will be enough of a triangle to work with on each side when I anchor the pocket. More important, I won't cut too much of the place-ment line, which would be visible on the right side of the garment.

My point here is to be aware that when you devitate from the basic textbook versions, lots of elements change. It's really important not to have the slash line show on the right side of the garment.

So draw the end lines, draw the triangles, and cut carefully. When you turn back the edge of the gar-ment along the slanted end line, you will see the base of an oddly shaped triangle—that's where you anchor the side of the slanted pocket!

POSITIONING A SLANTED POCKET

Wrong side

Stitching lines are offset.

Slash between stitching lines.

Right side

Wrong side

Fold back along the base of the triangle. Anchor the triangle separately from the pocket pieces.

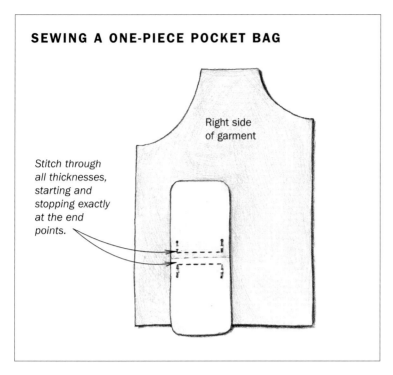

SEWING A ONE-PIECE POCKET BAG

Right side
of garment

Stitch through
all thicknesses,
starting and
stopping exactly
at the end
points.

19. Check one last time that the lips are straight and the pocket is flat. Sew across the base of the triangle on one end of the pocket, then stitch the edges of the pocket pieces together, sewing around the pocket bag to the other triangle. Sew along the base of the triangle on the second side.

20. Make a second row of stitches next to the first one around the pocket bag. Trim the edges so they are even. Sew additional rows of stitches across the triangles if you wish.

CONSTRUCTING AND USING A ONE-PIECE POCKET BAG

One alternative to using separate pocket pieces for the pocket back and the pocket front is the one-piece pocket bag. This is best used with a welt because the piece will be hidden by the welt and therefore can be constructed with pocketing or lining fabric. If your fabric is light in weight, you can construct this one-piece pocket bag with fashion fabric.

1. Cut a rectangle two times the depth of the pocket plus two seam allowances plus the width of the inset opening. Fold the piece in half and make little snips on each side to indicate the center of the rectangle.

2. Proceed through the welt pocket construction up to and including basting the welt upside down on the right side of the garment (see steps 1 through 4 and 9 on p. 69 and p. 70). If you are using a one-piece pocket bag for a single lip or buttonhole pocket, construct up to and including basting the lip or lips upside down on the right side of the garment. (For a single lip, follow steps 1 through 4 and 9 on p. 65 and p. 66; for a buttonhole pocket, follow steps 1 through 4 and 8 and 9 on p. 67.)

3. Working on the right side of the garment, with right sides together, position the one-piece pocket bag over the basted welt or lips, matching the center of the rectangle with the basted pocket-placement line.

4. Using the basting lines as a guide, stitch from end point to end point (see the drawing above).

5. Cut the rectangular piece along the center.

6. Continue the pocket construction process by cutting the garment along the pocket-placement line, clipping diagonally to make the triangles. Gently push all the fabric to the wrong side of the garment. Press and finish the ends of the pocket and the pocket bag, following steps 16 through 18 of the welt pocket construction (see pp. 71-72), steps 16 through 18 of the single-lip pocket construction (see p. 67), or steps 16 through 18 of the buttonhole pocket construction (see p. 69).

CONSTRUCTING A FACED ONE-PIECE POCKET BAG

Another one-piece pocket bag I see in men's tailoring and in my had-to-have silk twill trousers (yes, even sewers buy ready-to-wear) is the faced one-piece pocket bag. This has an area faced with fashion fabric so that it can be used under double-lip inset pockets—pockets in which the pocket back sometimes shows. This rectangle is two times the depth of the pocket plus seam allowances plus the width of the inset opening, and is usually constructed with pocketing or lining fabric. A 3-in. piece of fashion fabric is stitched to one end of the rectangle (this will become the pocket back). It is important to know the depth of the pocket since the piece will be folded at that point. I make small snips at each side to mark this foldline.

1. Complete construction of a double-lip buttonhole pocket up to the point when the lips have been slipstitched together with silk thread (see steps 1 through 12 on pp. 67-68 and the drawing below).

2. Now place the right side of the unfaced edge of the rectangular pocket piece against the stitching line that attaches the lower lip. Stitch.

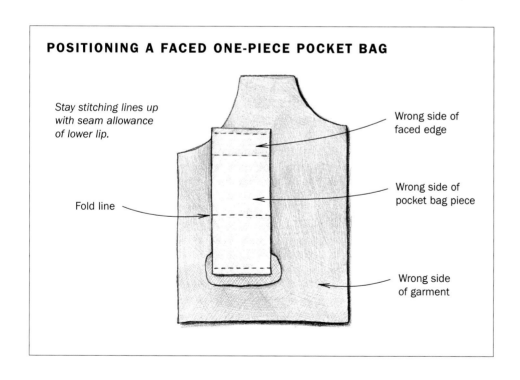

POSITIONING A FACED ONE-PIECE POCKET BAG

Stay stitching lines up with seam allowance of lower lip.

Fold line

Wrong side of faced edge

Wrong side of pocket bag piece

Wrong side of garment

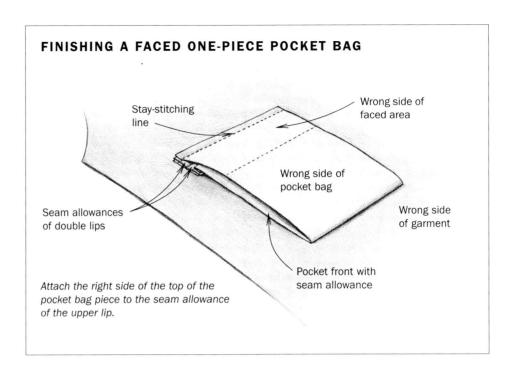

FINISHING A FACED ONE-PIECE POCKET BAG

Stay-stitching line

Wrong side of faced area

Wrong side of pocket bag

Seam allowances of double lips

Wrong side of garment

Pocket front with seam allowance

Attach the right side of the top of the pocket bag piece to the seam allowance of the upper lip.

3. Fold the piece, using the snips that marked the pocket depth as a guide. The rectangle will now be right sides together, with the faced section behind the inset opening. Attach the top edge along the attachment seam of the upper lip of the double-lip pocket (see the drawing above).

EMBELLISHING AN INSET POCKET WITH CORDING

Cording can consist of a "made" casing of bias fabric around a piece of yarn or cotton cord, or it can consist of a bought strip that combines a flat tape and a round cord. In both instances, the cord is somewhat loose or flexible unless the stitching is right up next to it. The trick is to end up without any of the loose or flexible part showing on the right side of the garment.

One of my great black jackets has cording along the edge of its shawl collar. In addition, each single-lip welt pocket has a strip of cording at the top. It's a challenge to construct this kind of detail, but it's worth it. I recommend sewing a sample before you try this on your garment!

1. Cording is attached to the pocket back piece. Uncurl the purchased cording or flatten the casing so that the cord itself can be positioned below the stay-stitching line along the top edge of the pocket back piece. Baste using a contrasting color thread. The basting line should be on top of the stay-stitching line and right next to the cord itself so that the cord is in a fixed position.

2. Attach the pocket back piece by sewing along the contrasting basting, using a zipper foot so that you can get right up next to the cord.

EMBELLISHING AN INSET POCKET BY STUFFING THE LIPS

I once saw a wonderful coat made out of a great designer fabric that featured fat double-lip pockets where the lips contained big cording. Using big cording is similar to adding cording detail: It is important to eliminate all the looseness in the casing so that the lips are stuffed tight when finished.

1. Cut bias strips of fabric wide enough to wrap around fat cord (you can find this cord in the upholstery section of most fabric stores). Wrap the cord with the bias strip and baste close enough to the cord to keep it in place, but not tight. For use in a double-lip buttonhole pocket, construct two pieces like this that are as wide as the pocket opening is long. To determine the width of the inset, line up the two stuffed lips close to each other and measure the width of the two stuffed pieces.

2. Generally you will follow the construction process for double-lip buttonhole pockets (see pp. 67-69). Position the stuffed lips on the right side of the garment parallel to the placement line. The raw edges of each stuffed casing should face the placement line. Baste each stuffed lip in place parallel to the pocket-placement line and half the width of the inset opening away from the placement line. You want to baste

Adding a Button/Button Loop

A great finish for a buttonhole pocket on the back of a pair of trousers is a button/button loop combination. The buttonhole, which can be on the lip or just under the pocket opening, is made after the pocket front is attached and through all layers of fabric, before the pocket bag is enclosed. The button will be attached to the pocket back after construction is completed. The loop can be a narrow tube or a tiny topstitched and folded piece, but it must be inserted between the garment fabric and the upper lip. This tiny piece is basted in place first to make sure it is long enough to reach the button, which is attached to the front of the garment after the construction is complete.

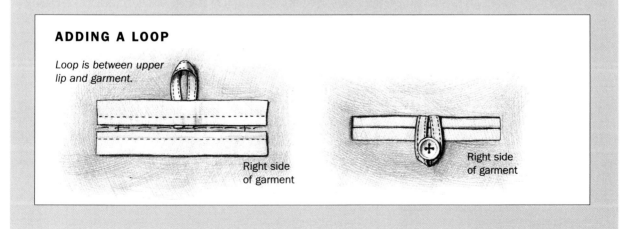

ADDING A LOOP

Loop is between upper lip and garment.

Right side of garment

Right side of garment

STUFFING THE LIPS

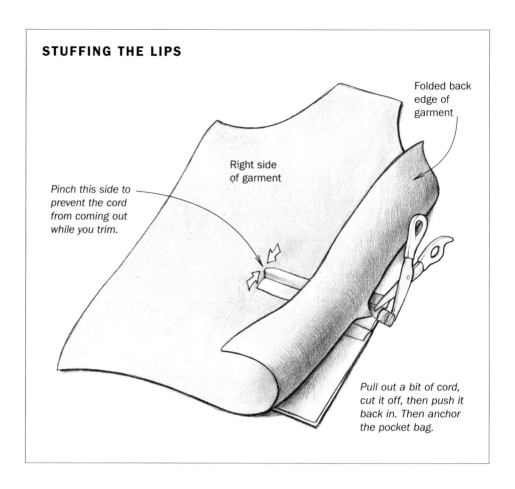

Folded back edge of garment

Right side of garment

Pinch this side to prevent the cord from coming out while you trim.

Pull out a bit of cord, cut it off, then push it back in. Then anchor the pocket bag.

close to the piece of fat cord inside the casings so that the lips are really stuffed when you flip them into place.

3. Check the basting lines from the wrong side of the garment to make sure they are straight and parallel. Tear out the stitches and rebaste if necessary.

4. On the right side of the garment, stitch the stuffed lips in place using a zipper foot so that you can get really close to the stuffing.

5. After the stuffed lips are attached, cut between the stitching lines and cut diagonally to the end of each stitching line, creating small triangles. Flip the lips into position, then attach the

pocket front and pocket back pieces, following steps 14 and 15 on pp. 68-69.

6. Turn the garment right side up and lay it flat on a table. Fold the garment back along the edge of the pocket. The small triangles should be visible over the edges of the stuffed lips. You need to remove the stuffing that is in the edges of the lips on the wrong side of the garment or else you'll have lumps under each end of your pocket. To do this, pinch the opposing end of the lip you are working on to keep the cord from coming out. Pull on the other end and trim away just the excess amount of cord. Push the cord back toward the lip (see the drawing on the facing page). Baste along the base of the triangle on this end of the pocket. Repeat for the other end.

7. Go back and securely stitch across the base of the triangle and around the pocket bag to the other side. Secure the triangle on the other side. Sew a second row of stitches around the pocket bag.

FINISHING THE RAW EDGES OF A WELT POCKET

It is possible to make a welt pocket in an unlined jacket, but you will have to decide how nice you want the inside of your garment to look. What will show inside will be the pocket, with a little bit of interfacing around the top. If you know you are not going to line the jacket, make that oval of interfacing a bit narrower and shorter than usual—a scant ¼ in. larger than the inset opening.

The edges of the pocket bag can be overlocked with a serger, but if your fabric is lightweight, those multiple rows of stitches may show through on the right side when the garment is pressed. There are pocket techniques for a clean-finished welt pocket, but binding the edges is also a good option.

For binding you will need enough double-fold bias to go around the entire pocket. Miter the edges for neat square corners, or simply curve the bias tape around the seam allowances for an easier, quicker application. (For more on this, see pp. 40-41.)

CURVING A WELT POCKET

Curving a welt pocket is a fabulous way to add interest to a garment. This pocket, however, is not for the faint of heart—it took me a long time to figure out just what I was supposed to do and a lot of practice to get one to look good. Many of the "rules" for this pocket are the opposite of what you do with other welt pockets.

There are two keys to making great curved pockets: Keeping the lips narrow and gently curving the pocket.

Think about those times you hemmed a circle skirt or an A-line skirt—remember how you had to fuss to turn a bigger circle under against a smaller circle? This is the challenge here. Narrow lips (or a narrow welt) work. The same is true for the gentle curve. Don't, as I did, think you can trace the edge of a butter plate and put a welt pocket in that curve! Find a pattern that has a curve, trace it, and keep it in your repertoire.

My advice continues. Stick to a single lip if at all possible, or if you must have a double-lip welt pocket, use very narrow lips—¼ in. would be best. A single lip of ½ in. is a good finished width for this pocket style.

1. Cut the lip from bias fabric. For a finished lip of ½ in., cut a bias strip 2 in. wide and as long as the opening plus 1½ in. Press the stretch out of the bias before using it—remember that a bias piece will get longer and narrower as you press out the stretch. Recut the strip so that it is even. It should measure two times the finished width of the lip plus seam allowances and a bit, and the finished length of the opening plus 1½ in. So a 5-in. pocket with a ½-in. finished lip would need a strip 1¾ in. by 6½ in.

CURVING A WELT POCKET

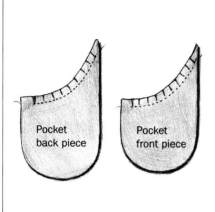

Pocket back piece

Pocket front piece

1. Make the pocket pieces by following the shape of a curve. Stay-stitch ¼ in. from the curved edge and clip seam allowances.

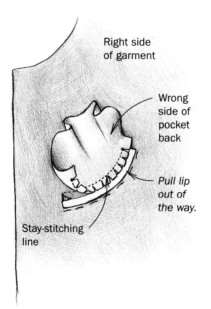

Wrong side of garment

Stay-stitch the inset.

Interfacing

2. Draw the curved rectangle, then stitch where you have drawn.

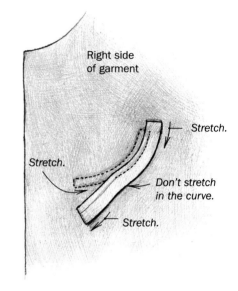

Right side of garment

Stretch.

Stretch.

Don't stretch in the curve.

Stretch.

3. Stitch the bias strip, matching a chalkline of the strip to the lower edge of the curve.

Right side of garment

Wrong side of pocket back

Pull lip out of the way.

Stay-stitching line

6. Match the stay-stitching lines of the pocket back piece and top of the inset. Pin, then sew, leaving ¾ in. unsewn at each end.

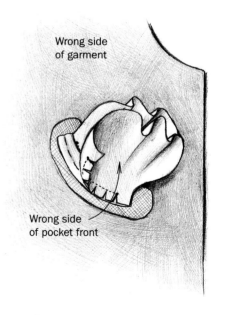

Wrong side of garment

Wrong side of pocket front

7. Sew the pocket front piece, matching the stay stitching to the seam allowance of the lip/strip.

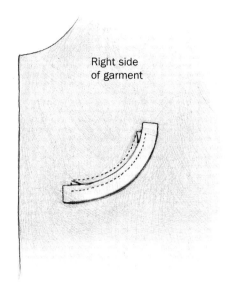

Right side
of garment

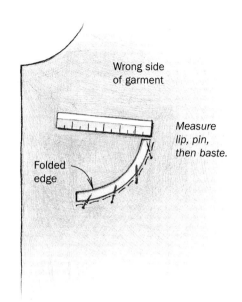

Wrong side
of garment

Measure
lip, pin,
then baste.

Folded
edge

4. Cut down the center of the curved rectangle, stopping ¾ in. from each end. Cut triangles to but not through each corner.

5. Push the strip through to the wrong side. Measure from the folded edge to make sure the lip fills the opening. Pin and baste.

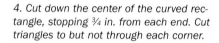

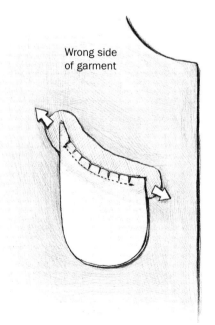

Wrong side
of garment

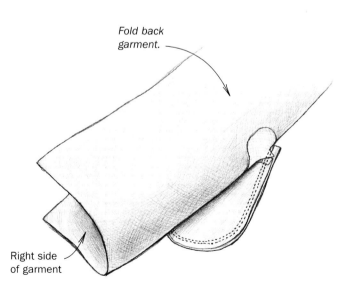

Fold back
garment.

Right side
of garment

8. Pull the pieces to the wrong side and line them up.

9. Anchor the base of the triangles and stitch around the pocket bag.

2. Mark a ½-in. line along one long edge of the strip using chalk or a pencil.
3. Cut the pocket pieces to match the garment. The curve is the top of the pocket, and both the pocket back and pocket front pieces must have the same curve, plus a ½-in. top seam allowance and ¾-in. side seam allowances. The pocket bag will hang below the curving line, generally on the straight grain. As with other pockets, the pocket bag should be as large as you need it to be for the style of garment you are making. On a jacket, the pocket bag should be large enough to accommodate your hand, but on a blouse or shirt, a less generous size is okay.

4. Stitch ½ in. from the top edge of each of these pocket pieces. Trim to ¼ in., then snip to but not through the stitching line at regular intervals.
5. Prepare the garment by first interfacing the wrong side in the area where the pocket will be constructed. Then trace the shape of the pocket onto the interfacing. Rather than just drawing a line, draw the curved rectangle, which is the inset opening, onto the wrong side of the garment. I will admit that I, the purist who bastes everything, have found tracing paper and a tracing wheel to work best for this. I then take my small ruler and a non-penetrating marker and correct the

tracing lines so that the curved lines of the box are an even width.

6. Now stay-stitch the shape of the box, using small stitches and thread with a good color match.

7. Next attach the lip. With the right side of the strip against the right side of the garment, stitch the bias strip in place along the lower line of the stitched box you have sewn on the garment. This is tricky. Leave ¾ in. free on each end. Start sewing exactly at one end of the stay-stitching line. Sew the bias strip ¼ in. from the edge, and tug the strip a bit in the sort-of-straight areas of the curve. Don't tug the bias strip in the curved areas, as this will cause it to curve in too much.

8. Once you have attached the lip, you get to cut! Start in the center of the box and cut down the middle as evenly as you can, stopping about ¾ in. from each end. Then clip to but not through each corner. You will have those nice triangles just like other welt pockets.

9. Push the unattached edge of the lip to the wrong side of the garment through the opening, wrapping the bias strip over the seam allowances, and pin in place along the seam line. It's now time to fuss (if you haven't been fussing yet). Measure the lip and make sure that it fits in the inset opening. Pin and baste. Then stitch in the ditch from the right side of the fabric along the seam line.

10. Attach the pocket back piece next. Working on the right side of the garment, with right sides together, position the pocket back piece on the garment so that the stay-stitching line at the top of the piece is along the stay-stitching line of the inset opening rectangle sewn on the garment. The small snips in the seam allowance will allow you to match the curve of the pocket back piece to the stay stitching on the garment. Pin this piece in place. Then check to see that you have positioned it correctly. Sew, leaving ¾ in. free on each end.

11. Attach the pocket front piece to the bias strip below the stitch-in-the-ditch line on the wrong side of the garment. Again, I recommend pinning the piece in place and checking the placement before sewing (can you tell where I've had problems?). Be careful to sew the right side of the pocket front piece to the lip seam allowances so that they will be between the garment and the wrong side of the pocket front piece. You don't want the seam allowance to be inside your pocket.

12. Push the pocket back piece to the wrong side of the garment. Turn the triangles toward the edges of the pockets. On the right side of the garment, whipstitch the top of the lip to the top of the inset opening. Press and pound.

13. Finish the rest of the pocket like a regular welt pocket: Place the garment right side up on a flat surface and fold back the garment in line with the base of the triangle. Give the edges of the bias strip a tug on each side to flatten the lips. Then baste along the base of the triangles to anchor the pocket in position.

14. Sew along the base of the triangle on one side of the pocket; sew the pocket back and pocket front pieces together around the pocket bag to the other triangle. Then sew along the base of the triangle on the other side. Make a second row of stitches next to the first one around the pocket bag. Finally trim the edges so they are even. If you wish, sew additional rows of stitches across the triangles.

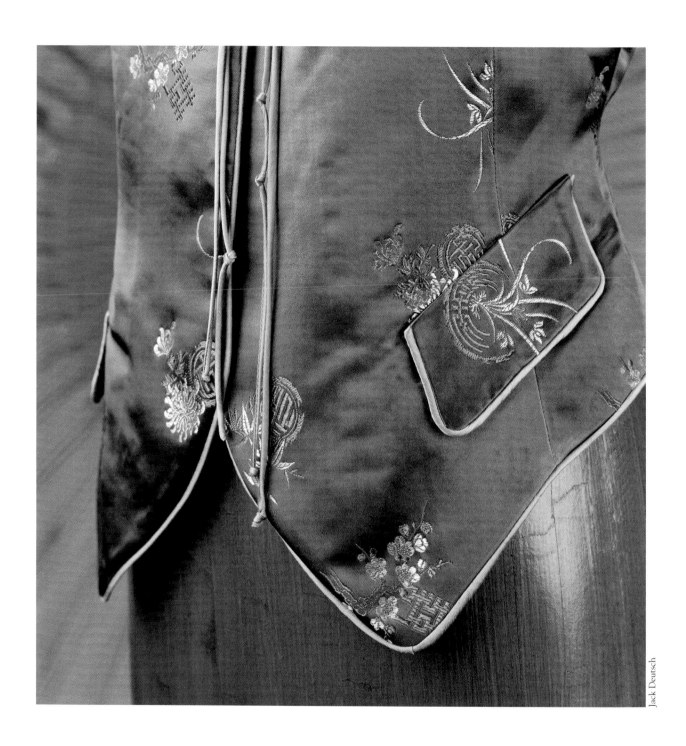

HIDDEN POCKETS

There are a handful of pockets that defy categorization. They are the hidden pockets—the patch pockets, in-seam pockets, and inset pockets whose openings are hidden under, near, or inside a pocket, a seam, or a garment. The first of these are what I call the fabulous fakes—welts and flaps that can hide pockets—or not! But there are other jewels I've saved for the back of the book, too. Included are the breast pocket; the ticket, or lipstick, pocket; the coin pocket; and the zippered welt pocket.

Constructing a Welt/Flap

Welts are the rectangular or shaped flaps that are found incorporated into some patch, in-seam, and inset pockets. For clarity, let's define welts as the pieces that are positioned "up" on a garment, attached at the bottom edge with the opening toward the top of the garment. Flaps, which are often shaped, will be defined as hanging toward the hem of the garment (see the drawing below). The construction is similar.

If you're making a mock pocket, mark the end points of the mock pocket on the garment with silk thread tailor tacks. On the wrong side of the garment, position an oval of fusible interfacing in the faux pocket area and fuse in place. Mark a line using a pencil or other non-penetrating marker. Then draw the end lines. Using silk thread, baste along the placement line and end lines as done in welt pocket construction, as shown in the bottom photo on p. 59.

Interface one of the welt/flap pieces: This will be the upper welt/flap piece, which is the one that will show from the right side of the garment. Trim ⅛ in. from three sides of the under welt, leaving the one long attachment edge untrimmed.

There are two common methods for constructing welts and flaps. The first is the method that I, who loves to make jackets, use most often since I like the look of flaps but don't like bulky ones. I use lining fabric for the under flap and consistently get good results. The second construction method is the one I use with mock welt pockets or flaps over patch pockets. This method includes a quick step for eliminating bulk at the point of attachment. Use this method if you are a beginning pocket maker.

WELTS AND FLAPS

Welt

Flap

Welts open toward the top of the garment.

Flaps hang toward the hem of the garment.

CONSTRUCTION METHOD 1

1. With right sides together, sew the upper welt/flap to the under welt/flap using a ⅝-in. seam allowance and taking care to match the edges of the pieces, even though the under welt/flap is a bit smaller.

2. Trim the seam allowances to ¼ in. Turn the welt/flap right side out. Use a point turner to push the edges into

Cording or Piping the Welt/Flap

A great way to jazz up a welt or flap is by adding cording or piping to the edges of the piece. This process adds a bit of time to the process of constructing the welt, but I have found the results are worth the extra effort (see the photo on p. 86).

Before you sew

Interface one of the welt/flap pieces: This will be the upper welt/flap. Trim ⅛ in. from three sides of the under welt, leaving one long attachment edge untrimmed.

Attaching the cording

1. Before attaching the upper welt/flap to the lower welt/flap, place the cording or piping around the edges of the upper welt/flap on the right side of the piece, matching the welt/flap seam allowances with the raw edges of the casing. Check to make sure that the cording will be tight inside its casing and right on the edge of the upper welt/flap when construction is complete. Baste.

2. Sew the upper welt/flap to the under welt/flap, taking care to match the edges even though the under welt/flap is a bit smaller. You can ease-stitch these pieces by sewing with the upper welt/flap on bottom. Since the upper welt/flap is longer, the sewing machine's feed dogs will draw this side up more, making easing easy.

3. Trim away the excess seam allowances, and turn the welt/flap to the right side. Press. The piece should look fabulous.

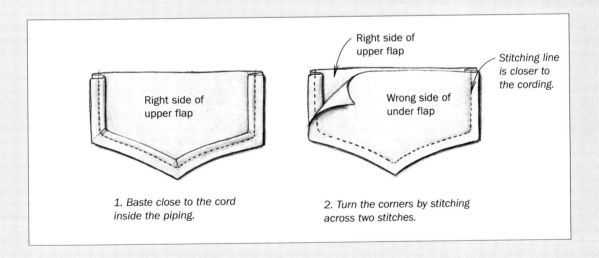

Right side of upper flap

Right side of upper flap

Wrong side of under flap

Stitching line is closer to the cording.

1. Baste close to the cord inside the piping.

2. Turn the corners by stitching across two stitches.

shape. Press, pounding flat with a clapper (this is an important step in the construction process of a welt or flap). If you are constructing a garment with two welt/flap pockets, compare the pieces now to make sure they are the same size and shape. Correct if necessary.

3. Topstitch now if you so choose. If the flap will have a button closure, or even a mock button closure, make the buttonhole in the flap now, too.

POSITIONING THE FLAP

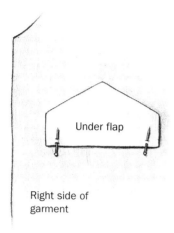

1. Pin the flap in place.

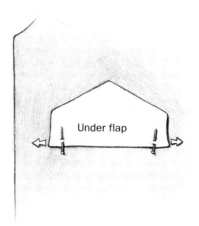

2. Pull out the ends ⅛ in. on each side and repin.

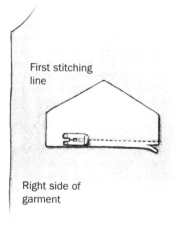

3. Ease-stitch the flap in place with the flap up, then sew a second row of stitches close to the first.

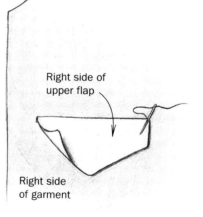

4. Trim the excess seam allowance, and press the flap down into position. Slipstitch the flap ends ⅜ in. on each side.

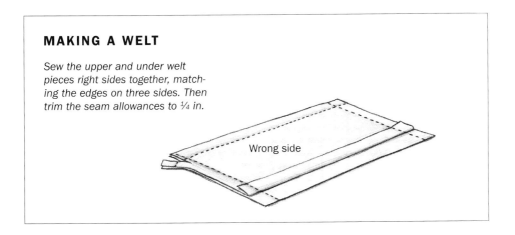

MAKING A WELT

Sew the upper and under welt pieces right sides together, matching the edges on three sides. Then trim the seam allowances to ¼ in.

Wrong side

ATTACHING THE WELT/FLAP METHOD 1

1. To attach the flap, place the unsewn edge of the flap against the top of the pocket or along the basted pocket-placement line. If you are using the welt/flap to hide the top of a patch pocket, the welt/flap is wider than the pocket by about ½ in. Center the flap above the pocket so that it extends evenly on each side of the pocket (see the drawing on the facing page). Pin and baste in place.

2. Now, so that the flap doesn't stand away from the garment, carefully pull each end out a bit (⅛ in. to ¼ in.) and repin securely. Ease-stitch the flap in place, with the flap side up. Sew a second row of stitches close to the attachment seam you have just sewn.

3. Trim the excess seam allowance with small, sharp scissors. Press the flap down over the stitching.

4. Slipstitch the ends of the flap about ⅜ in. down on each side to cover the attachment stitches.

CONSTRUCTION METHOD 2

1. Press the ⅝-in. seam allowance on the upper welt/flap to the wrong side, then trim to ⅜ in.

2. With right sides together, sew the upper welt/flap to the under welt/flap along the remaining edges, using a ⅝-in. seam allowance and taking care to match these edges even though the under welt/flap is a bit smaller (see the drawing above).

3. Trim the seam allowances to ¼ in. Turn the welt/flap right side out and press. Pound with a clapper to flatten the piece. Use a point turner to push the corners into shape. Topstitch the welt now if you so choose. Add buttonholes if needed.

ATTACHING THE WELT/FLAP METHOD 2

1. Working on the right side of the garment with right sides together, position the welt upside down (see the drawing on p. 92). The welt's ⅝-in. seam allowance will be along the basted pocket-placement line. In other words, if the finished mock pocket is open at the top, position the welt so that the unsewn seam allowance is toward the top of the garment with the finished edge toward the hem of the garment. If the finished garment features a decorative flap, position the flap so that the unsewn seam allowance is toward the hem of the garment, right side of the flap against the right side of the garment, with the finished edges of the flap toward the top of the garment.

2. Pin and baste the welt/flap in place from end point to end point, matching the seam line to the basted line on the garment. Before you sew, pull the ends of the welt out a bit, ⅛ in. to ¼ in., on each side. Ease-stitch the piece into position. This will prevent the welt from standing away from the garment. Sew a second row of stitches parallel to the first, about ¼ in. away.

3. Trim the seam allowance close to the second row of stitches.

4. Slipstitch the foldline of the pressed-back seam allowance close to the attachment stitching. This method eliminates the bulk of sewing through two layers of fabric.

5. Press the mock pocket welt up over the stitching line toward the top of the garment if the opening is toward the top of the garment or press it toward the hem if the opening is from below. To attach the mock pocket along the short edges, either machine-stitch the edges in place or hand-stitch. To hand-stitch, pin or pin and baste the welt into position. From the wrong side of the garment, use small, diagonal stitches to anchor the edges of the welt, taking care not to pull the stitches too tight. Press the finished mock pocket.

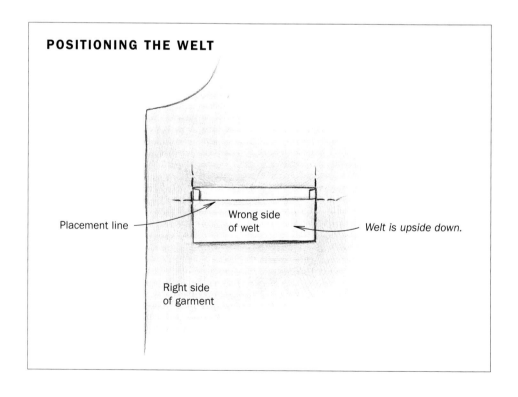

POSITIONING THE WELT

Placement line

Wrong side of welt

Welt is upside down.

Right side of garment

6. For a flap, press down over the stitching toward the hem of the garment. Slipstitch the ends of the flap about ⅜ in. on each side to hide the seam allowances, or use small diagonal stitches on the wrong side of the garment to anchor the sides of the flap.

BREAST POCKET

A breast pocket is a common feature in men's suits but not in ladies' suits. However, a sewing student of mine came to class in a fabulous little jacket by a local designer. The jacket was short with a simple collar and no visible pocket. The inside of the jacket was another story—there was a low welt pocket made of striped lining fabric—nothing to detract from the simple lines of the garment. It was just the right size pocket for what I call evening essentials: a handkerchief, I.D., and cab fare, or a lipstick (see the photo below).

This pocket is easily replicated. Whereas this pocket is high on a man's suit—truly a breast pocket—a lower pocket is better suited to a lady's garment and figure. The pocket is constructed inside the jacket front, across both the front facing and the lining. Since it is easier to construct an inset pocket on a flat piece of fabric, the pocket is constructed after the lining is attached along the facing edge, but before the lining is attached to either the jacket sleeves or the hem.

A breast pocket is constructed inside the jacket front, across the front facing and lining. For a ladies' garment, construct it about 2 in. to 3 in. below the armhole. (Photo by Jack Deutsch.)

BEFORE YOU SEW

Mark each end of the placement line with silk thread tailor tacks. Then interface the pocket-placement line on the wrong side of the facing/lining piece by fusing an oval of interfacing over the placement line.

Working on the wrong side of the facing/lining piece, mark a line on the fusible interfacing between the tailor tacks using a pencil or other non-penetrating marker. Draw the end lines, too. Using silk thread, baste along the line and end markings. Make your stitches even so that you can see the markings on both the right side and the wrong side of the fabric.

You only need to make this pocket on one side of the garment (I don't think it matters which side), so you can take extra time and have some fun by making the lip on the bias (see p. 66) or by adding a button closure (see p. 79).

SEWING A BREAST POCKET

1. Prepare the lip by folding it in half and pressing, pressing, pressing. Measure the finished width of the lip from the folded edge of the lip, and mark a line the full length of the lip. Stay-stitch along this line. Trim the seam allowance to ¼ in.

2. Cut each pocket piece following the directions for a single-lip inset pocket (see pp. 65-67). To mark each pocket piece, sew a stay-stitching line ¼ in. from the edge all along one end of each piece.

3. Position the pieces on the right side of the facing/lining piece, with the lip below the basted placement line and the pocket back piece above the pocket-placement line. Pin and check that the

stay-stitching lines are parallel and exactly as far apart as the finished width of the lip. Baste. Baste or pin the end marks.

4. Machine-stitch along the basting, stopping and starting exactly at the end marks.

5. Measure and check that your stitching lines are straight and parallel. Pull them out and resew if necessary.

6. From the wrong side of the facing/lining piece and using small, sharp scissors, cut along the pocket-placement line, stopping ¾ in. from each end line. Use your fingers to keep the seam allowances of the pocket back piece and lip out of the way of your scissors. Cut triangles to but not through each corner.

7. Push the pieces into position: The pocket back piece will hang toward the hem of the garment with its seam allowance pressed up. The lip will "sit up" in the inset opening, with its seam allowance pressed toward the hem.

8. Attach the pocket front piece on the wrong side of the garment. Match the stay-stitching line to the seam allowance of the lip so that the seam allowance of the lip is between the garment and the wrong side of the pocket front piece.

9. Tug a bit on both lips to pull the pieces into position. Make sure the small triangles are pointing toward each side and sitting neatly on top of the seam allowances of the lip and pocket pieces. On the right side of the garment and with silk thread, slipstitch the top edge of the lip along the top of the inset opening.

10. Press and pound the lip from the right side.

11. From the right side of the facing/lining piece, fold the garment back in line with the end of the pocket. Machine-baste along the base of the triangle, through all thicknesses, and along the side of the pocket pieces. Repeat for the other end of the pocket.

12. Sew a second row of stitches across the base of the triangle and around the pocket. Trim away uneven edges and excess fabric.

TICKET POCKET

A ticket pocket is a small rectangular patch pocket stitched inside any larger pocket—but especially good in an inset pocket. The patch can really be ticket size: 2 in. wide by 3 in. long. Posi-

tion the ticket pocket about ¾ in. to 1 in. below the opening of the pocket. This allows easy access to it but hides it from view.

A ticket pocket is also a great addition to a breast pocket. Just attach the small patch to the pocket back piece before constructing the inset pocket. And it's just the right size for a lipstick!

SEWING A TICKET POCKET

1. Create this hidden pocket as an unlined patch pocket. Cut the rectangle to the desired size plus seam allowances and top foldback facing—our 2-in. by 3-in. ticket pocket would be 3¼ in. by 4¾ in. Mark each end of the foldback line with tiny snips.

A ticket pocket—a small rectangular patch—can be added inside any larger pocket.

2. Turn ¼ in. of the foldback facing to the wrong side and stitch.

3. Press the foldback facing to the right side of the patch, using the snips as a guide. Sew around the pocket, anchoring the foldback on both sides and creating a stay-stitching line around the remainder of the pocket.

4. Trim the excess fabric from the foldback area and turn right side out.

Clip straight into the seam allowances so that the pocket piece can be completely flipped to the wrong side of the garment.

Press the pocket piece to the wrong side of the garment.

Use a point turner to push the corners into shape.

5. Press the seam allowances to the wrong side of the patch all around.

6. Pin or pin and baste the patch in position on the right side of the garment. Stitch close to the edge of the pocket, anchoring both top corners.

Coin Pocket

Although a ticket pocket in a jacket is often considered a coin pocket, a coin pocket in slacks is located just under the waistband and can be partly covered by a slant-front pocket, like in your jeans (see the bottom photo on the facing page). Here is another good place to stash some cash!

A coin pocket is constructed in the side front piece of a slant-front pocket or in the garment front piece of a side-seam pocket. The opening is only about 2 in. wide. This pocket is easily constructed with a single rectangular piece 3 in. wide and 5½ in. long for a 2-in. finished depth. I suggest constructing the piece with lining or pocketing fabric and facing the rectangle with a piece of fashion fabric. Baste a 2-in. piece of fashion fabric to the rectangle along one end. Turn the other edge of the fashion fabric under and topstitch in place on the rectangle.

SEWING A COIN POCKET

1. Place the rectangle on the garment with the unfaced edge along the garment waistline edge.

2. Sew, leaving ⅝ in. on each side unattached.

3. Clip straight into the seam allowances (to but not through), as shown in the top photo on the facing page.

4. Press the pocket piece away from the garment over the seam allowances, then press against the wrong side of the garment (see the bottom photo on the facing page). If you wish, topstitch along the sewn edge of the pocket opening.

5. Now fold up the piece to make the pocket 2 in. deep (see the photo at right). Stitch along both unattached sides, taking care not to catch any of the pocket back piece.

If this pocket is like the one in your jeans, it is constructed in the garment side front/pocket back piece. Take care to center the piece so that it is not too close to the side seam and not covered too much by the pocket/garment front.

Fold the pocket piece up to form a 2-in.-deep pocket.

The top of the coin pocket will be attached to the waistband when the garment is finished.

Zippered Welt Pocket

The last fabulous hidden pocket is not really a pocket—it is a zipper closing in a pocket. Vests, jackets, and slacks can all be enhanced with double-lip inset pockets accessible through zippered openings—and I love the do-dads that can be hung from the zipper tabs. The key to constructing this closure is that the inset opening of the pocket that is closed with a zipper needs to be narrower than the zipper is wide. I find ¾ in. is the right size.

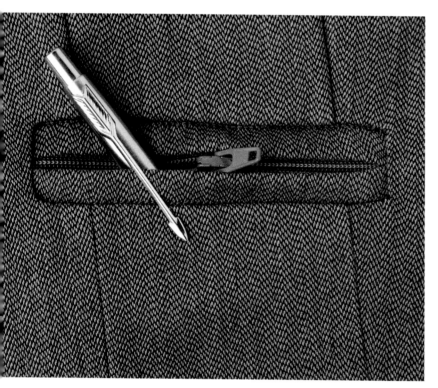

This double-lip inset pocket has ⅜-in.-wide lips—about the maximum width you can use. (Photo by Jack Deutsch.)

SEWING A ZIPPERED WELT POCKET

1. After constructing a double-lip inset pocket to the point that the lips are whipstitched together (see p. 68), place a short zipper on the wrong side of the fabric, under the lips. Center the zipper teeth directly under the whip-stitching along the line where the lips meet (see the top photo on the facing page).

2. Baste the zipper in place. Check to make sure that you can attach the zipper tape on both sides by stitching in the ditch from the right side of the garment. Then sew (see the center photo on the facing page).

3. Secure the ends of the zipper in the finishing that secures the lips, the tiny triangles, and the pocket bag pieces, with two caveats: The zipper stop needs to be away from the base of the triangle or you will break the needle trying to sew over it (see the bottom photo on the facing page). And the zipper pull needs to be inside the inset when you secure this end of the pocket, or you won't be able to open the zipper. Pulling the zipper partly open before anchoring solves this problem.

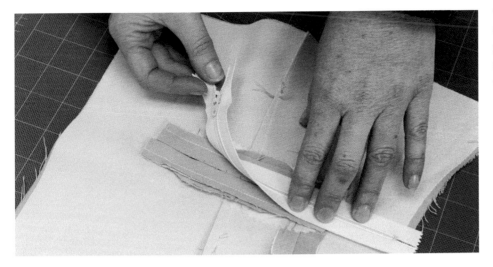

When adding the zipper to a double-lip inset pocket, place the zipper teeth along the center of the two lips.

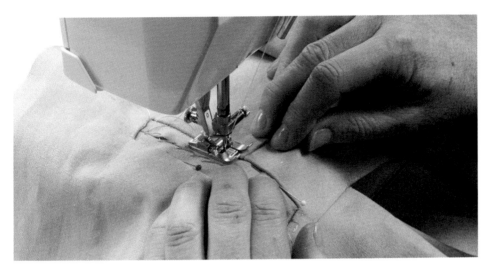

From the right side of the garment, stitch in the ditch along the seam lines to attach the zipper.

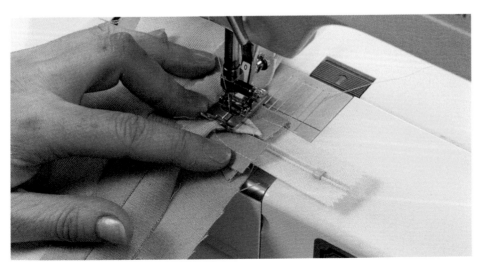

Finish the pocket, sewing over the ends of the zipper tape. Make sure the zipper stop is out of the way!

RESOURCES

Apparel Component Supply/A.C.S.
447 W. 36th St.
New York, NY 10018
(800) 739-8783
FAX (212) 947-9281
Tailoring supplies, including lining
materials and pocketing. Catalog
available.

Baer Fabrics
515 E. Market St.
Louisville, KY 40202
(800) 769-7776, (502) 569-7010
FAX (502) 582-2331
Tailoring supplies and fabric, including
Bemberg rayon. Catalog available.

Britex Fabrics
146 Geary St.
San Francisco, CA 94108
(415) 392-2910
Retail store and mail order fabrics,
trims, and buttons.

G Street Fabrics
11854 Rockville Pike
Rockville, MD 20852
(301) 231-8998
Bemberg rayon.

G Street Mail Order Services
12240 Wilkins Ave.
Rockville, MD 20852
(800) 333-9191
Quality fabrics, notions, trims, and
accessories. Swatching service.

HE-RO Sewing Center
495 S. Clinton Ave.
Rochester, NY 14620
(800) 739-9464, (716) 232-2160
Tailoring supplies, including pocketing
and Bemberg rayon. Catalog available.

Oregon Tailor Supply Co.
2123 S.E. Division St.
P.O. Box 42284
Portland, OR 97242
(800) 678-2457, (503) 232-6191
FAX (503) 232-9470
Sewing, tailoring, and dressmaking sup-
plies and trims. Catalog available.

Sawyer Brook Distinctive Fabrics
P.O. Box 1800
Clinton, MA 01510-0813
(800) 290-2739, (508) 368-3133
Mail order fabric, including Bemberg
rayon.

Things Japanese
9805 N.E. 116th St., Suite 7160
Kirkland, WA 98034-4248
(206) 821-2287
FAX (206) 821-3554
Silk thread. Catalog available.

Wawak Corp.
2235 Hammond Dr.
Schaumburg, IL 60173
(800) 654-2235, (847) 397-4850
Tailoring supplies, linings, and buttons.
Catalog available.

INDEX

Book Publisher: Jim Childs

Acquisitions Editor: Jolynn Gower

Publishing Coordinator: Sarah Coe

Editors: Anne Brennan, Carolyn Mandarano

Layout Artist: Thomas Lawton

Photographers: Jack Deutsch, Scott Phillips

Illustrator: Robert La Pointe

Indexer: Tom McKenna

Typeface: Goudy

Paper: 70-lb. Patina

Printer: Quebecor Printing/Hawkins, Church Hill, Tennessee